Home Office Research Study 245

Improving public attitudes to the Criminal Justice System: The impact of information

Becca Chapman, Catriona Mirrlees-Black and Claire Brawn

The views expressed in this report are those of the authors, not necessarily those of the Home Office (nor do they reflect Government policy).

Home Office Research, Development and Statistics Directorate
July 2002

Home Office Research Studies

The Home Office Research Studies are reports on research undertaken by or on behalf of the Home Office. They cover the range of subjects for which the Home Secretary has responsibility. Other publications produced by the Research, Development and Statistics Directorate include Findings, Statistical Bulletins and Statistical Papers.

The Research, Development and Statistics Directorate

RDS is part of the Home Office. The Home Office's purpose is to build a safe, just and tolerant society in which the rights and responsibilities of individuals, families and communities are properly balanced and the protection and security of the public are maintained.

RDS is also part of National Statistics (NS). One of the aims of NS is to inform Parliament and the citizen about the state of the nation and provide a window on the work and performance of government, allowing the impact of government policies and actions to be assessed.

Therefore –

Research Development and Statistics Directorate exists to improve policy making, decision taking and practice in support of the Home Office purpose and aims, to provide the public and Parliament with information necessary for informed debate and to publish information for future use.

First published 2002

ISBN 1 84082 851 X
ISSN 0072 6435

Foreword

Successive sweeps of the British Crime Survey (BCS) and other surveys have shown how poorly informed the public are about crime, the operation of the criminal justice system (CJS) and sentencing in particular. Furthermore, those who are worst informed hold the most negative views about the CJS, and those who are best informed tend to have greater confidence in most aspects of the system.

This previous work demonstrates a correlational relationship between knowledge and attitudes, but not a causal one. The aim of the research reported here was to determine whether providing information would have an effect on levels of knowledge; whether any improvement in knowledge would have a direct impact on attitudes; and which of three methods of presentation would be the most efficient and effective at imparting information to the public.

The indications of this small-scale study are that public knowledge of the CJS can be improved by a range of methods. Each mode of communication had differential effects on attitudes, but each tended to improve satisfaction with at least some aspects of the system. Of those modes of communication trialed, a specially designed booklet was as effective a method as the others and considerably cheaper. On the available evidence it also appeared to reach a wider audience. The booklet has now been revised in the light of the research and has been made widely available.

David Moxon
Crime and Criminal Justice Unit

Acknowledgements

Firstly, thanks are due to those members of the public who gave up their time to participate in this research.

The research was organised and the interviews conducted by Taylor Nelson Sofres. Particular thanks go to Neil Russell, Katherine Davis and Cynthia Pinto and to Professor Rod Morgan who provided consultancy support and chaired the seminars.

The Prison Service presentations at the seminars were given by Gareth Davies, Louise Taylor, John Thomas and Danny McAlister. Mark Harris, Stewart McPhillips, Granville Brunt and Matthew Kelley were the presenters from the Probation Service. We are very grateful for the time and thought they put into the presentations and the question and answer sessions.

The booklet was produced by Eaglevision and Appetite and printed by Printflow.

The video was developed and produced by Eaglevision.

This research was commissioned by the Sentencing Review team. We are grateful to John Halliday and Cecilia French for their input and interest in its development and findings.

A number of Home Office colleagues contributed to the development of this work. Particular thanks go to Pat Dowdeswell and Victoria Richardson.

Julian Roberts of the University of Ottawa and Mark Ormerod provided very helpful reviews in the final stages of writing this report.

Becca Chapman
Catriona Mirrlees-Black
Claire Brawn

Contents

List of tables

List of figures

Appendix tables

Summary

Building on previous research evidence that attitudes towards the criminal justice system (CJS) are related to knowledge about the system, the aim of this work was to determine:

- whether providing information has an effect on levels of public knowledge;
- whether any improvements in knowledge that result have an impact on attitudes and confidence in the CJS;
- which of three methods of presentation of information would be the most efficient and effective for imparting information to the public.

The research surveyed a nationally representative sample of 1022 people to assess levels of knowledge about crime, sentencing and the CJS; attitudes to sentencing; and confidence in the CJS. Of these, 220 then participated in an experiment to test the impact of providing information.

Three formats were tested, all containing the same key facts about crime and the criminal justice system:

- 109 people were given a 24-page booklet designed to be visually attractive and easy to understand;
- 37 attended seminars involving presentations by experts, and question and answer sessions; and
- 74 watched a video combining footage of one of the seminars with other visual material.

The 220 were then reinterviewed to assess what impact participation had had on their levels of knowledge and attitudes to the CJS.

Knowledge of crime and the criminal justice system

- Overall knowledge about crime and the criminal justice system amongst the general public is poor. There is particularly poor knowledge about crime trends and current sentencing practice. In line with previous research, most people believed crime was going up (over a period when it was falling), and the use of custody in sentencing was considerably underestimated.

- There was little systematic variation in knowledge by demographic characteristics, although men and people of working age tend to be slightly more knowledgeable. People who have had contact with the criminal justice system, who are interested in law and order issues and those with some educational qualifications also tend to be better informed.
- After receiving information, participants increased the number of questions they answered correctly. All three formats significantly improved knowledge scores. There was some evidence that information that is surprising, or repeated, is more likely to be recalled.
- Those who had the lowest initial levels of knowledge were the most likely to increase the number of questions they answered correctly after receiving information. People with a demonstrated ability to learn and gain educational qualifications performed better than average.

Sentencing aims and practices

- Crime reduction was most frequently mentioned as the 'most important' aim of sentencing. When asked to choose between seven aims of sentencing, 'changing behaviour to prevent re-offending' was chosen by the largest number of people.
- There were few changes in preferences for the main aim of sentencing after receiving information. The largest shift was in the proportion of those who had watched the video who thought punishment should be the main aim of sentencing, but this was not statistically significant.
- There was a widespread belief in the effectiveness of prison at reducing crime, and in achieving other aims of sentencing. After receiving information, there were some increases in support for alternative disposals, but the ratings for prison also increased, and by a greater amount.
- When sentencing a typical case, respondents' use of custody for both burglars and robbers was considerably lower than the rates of custody given by the courts for these types of cases. Sentencing did not change very much as a result of giving participants information.

Fear of crime, attitudes and confidence in the criminal justice system

- A reduction in worry about victimisation was found for all information formats. This effect was similar for most demographic groups. Those who were originally 'very worried' were the most likely to report a lower level of worry after receiving information, as were those who had educational qualifications.

- Providing information also had an effect on opinions about sentencing. Respondents were less likely to think sentencing was too lenient after receiving information. This effect was seen across all socio-demographic groups. Those who had initially thought sentences were 'much too lenient' were most likely to change. The shift in views was at least partly related to an improvement in knowledge. When asked why they had changed their views, many participants said that the information had prompted greater consideration of the issues, but others attributed it to events in the media and personal experience.
- There was also some impact on confidence in the criminal justice system. For confidence that the criminal justice system brings people who commit crimes to justice, those with poor confidence initially were most likely to improve in confidence. Those who had initially said they were very interested in law and order issues changed less than others.

Evaluation of the information sources

- Some types of people were more likely to participate in the research. For instance, those from minority ethnic communities and people with particularly poor levels of knowledge were less likely to participate in any of the three information groups. Those who attended the seminars were particularly unrepresentative of the general population: the better qualified and those very interested in law and order issues were most likely to attend. There was least evidence of any bias in participation for the booklet group.
- Generally, ratings of all the information sources were positive. All of the information formats were thought to be informative, interesting, enjoyable and helpful. The seminar was most positively rated on many of the evaluation questions.
- The booklet and video were both thought to be 'modern', and 'different' from other government publications. Generally, the sources were thought to be credible and accurate, although this was less so for the video. Respondents expressed surprise at many of the facts presented, and these were the facts that were particularly well recalled.
- Many respondents from all the groups reported that they had changed their views and that they were now more confident about the system, although the seminar had less impact here.

Conclusion

- Providing simple factual information improved knowledge about crime and sentencing, and also had an impact on attitudes to and confidence in the CJS, although the evidence for a direct relationship between improvements in knowledge and attitude change is less clear. All three of the information formats tested improved knowledge and had some influence on attitudes.
- Previous work to improve satisfaction and confidence in the criminal justice system has tended to concentrate on targeting victims, witnesses and those in contact with the system. The current research indicates that the widespread dissatisfaction and misunderstanding of the system amongst the general public can also be addressed.
- The booklet was the most cost-effective format tested and reached the widest cross-section of people. The booklet has therefore been updated and redesigned, taking into account the comments from the participants in the research. It is likely to form part of the strategy to improve confidence in the criminal justice system in England and Wales.

1 Introduction

The research reported here was commissioned by the Home Office team who conducted the 2000/2001 review of the sentencing framework. In the main the purpose of the work was to examine public attitudes to the current sentencing framework and to test out options for change. Because previous work had shown the public to be very badly informed about current sentencing practice, the review team was concerned about the value of public opinion as a means of informing change, if that opinion was based on misperceptions. For this reason it was decided to investigate the feasibility of improving public knowledge and monitoring the impact this had on their views. Three methods of improving public knowledge were tested: a booklet, a series of seminars, and a video. A full report of the general public's views on many aspects of the sentencing framework and options for change, was published in Appendix 5 of 'Making Punishments Work', the report of the review of the sentencing framework.[1]

A further impetus to this work was the government's objective of an improvement by 2004 in the level of public confidence in the criminal justice system (CJS). Confidence in the system is clearly important for maintaining public support for the rule of law. It is also key to ensuring the public play their role in the process as witnesses or jurors and are willing to participate as volunteers, for example as magistrates or on youth offending panels.

This report explores in greater depth the relationship between the format of information, knowledge and attitude change. Specifically:

- whether providing information has an effect on levels of public knowledge;
- whether any improvements in knowledge that result have an impact on attitudes and confidence in the CJS;
- which of three methods of presentation of information would be the most efficient and effective methods of imparting information to the public.

1. The analysis in 'Making Punishments Work' mainly compares the 1022 General Public Sample (GPS) and an 'Informed Public Sample' (IPS, N=92). The latter were those who answered seven or more questions correctly in the second survey. No findings from the IPS are given in this report.

Knowledge, attitudes about crime and sentencing, and confidence in the criminal justice system

Public opinion about some aspects of the CJS is poor. Although a majority of people are confident the CJS respects the rights of people accused of crime, less than half believe it is effective in bringing offenders to justice, dealing with cases efficiently or meeting the needs of victims. The courts and sentencers receive particularly low ratings (Mirrlees-Black, 2001). This is at least partly because most people think that sentencing is too lenient.[2 3]

However this is not to say the public are more punitive than the judiciary. When asked to select a sentence for a specific offence and offender, they tend to choose sentences which are broadly in line with, if not more lenient than, those used by sentencers (Hough and Roberts, 1998).[4] It appears that the perception of lenience results from a lack of awareness of the severity of the sentences given in court, and generally poor knowledge about criminal justice system procedures.[5] The general lack of confidence in the CJS also seems to be affected by misperceptions of the crime problem. People tend to think crime is rising a lot (even during periods when it is actually declining) and overestimate the proportion of crime that is violent.

People who are better informed about crime and sentencing tend to rate the CJS more highly. Hough and Roberts (1998) found that poor knowledge about crime and punishment was associated with more negative ratings of courts and sentencers. Mattinson and Mirrlees-Black (2000) confirmed a similar picture for perceptions of the youth justice system: those with low levels of knowledge were more likely to think that sentencing in the youth justice system was too lenient. And Mirrlees-Black (2001) found that misperceptions about crime trends and sentencing practice were related to lower levels of confidence in the CJS.

In theory, therefore, improving public knowledge about crime, sentencing and the CJS might be expected to result in more positive attitudes towards the CJS. Improvements in ratings of

2. In 1996, 51 per cent of those interviewed in the British Crime Survey thought sentencing was much too lenient, and 28 per cent a little too lenient. In 1998, the figures were 49 per cent and 30 per cent respectively.
   The British Social Attitudes Survey has measured punitiveness since 1986. In this time, the proportion of respondents agreeing strongly with the statement 'People who break the law should be given stiffer sentences' has varied, being generally between 27 per cent and 33 per cent in the late 80s, falling to 20 per cent in 1991, and rising to 41 per cent in 1993, before returning to similar levels in 1994 to 1996 as seen in 1986 to 1990.
3. A survey in Scotland produced similar findings: Anderson, Ingram & Hutton (2002).
4. This has been found for burglary by Hough & Roberts (1998) and Russell & Morgan (2001). Hough (1996) found court of appeal judgements to be acceptable to the majority of groups of members of the public for seven out of nine offences including burglary, actual bodily harm and shoplifting.
5. Lack of knowledge about sentences given by the courts has been found by a number of studies, including Hough & Moxon (1985), Hough & Roberts (1998) and Mattinson and Mirrlees-Black (2000).

the system should be achievable where current opinion is based on overly negative beliefs. There is, however, little known about whether it is possible to influence knowledge, attitudes and confidence in the CJS by providing information.

Can information have an impact on attitudes?

There is little research looking at whether information campaigns change public knowledge and attitudes in the field of criminal justice. Most of what does exist relates to crime prevention campaigns, which have a particular behavioural aim. However, some of these also evaluate changes in knowledge and attitudes.

In the US, the National Crime Prevention Council evaluated their long running 'McGruff' crime prevention campaign. The NCPC found that a quarter of those interviewed reported having learnt something new from the crime prevention campaign (O'Keefe *et al*, 1996). A further half reported being reminded of things they had forgotten. Riley and Mayhew (1980) found a high level of recognition of the slogans associated with press and television campaigns aimed at promoting household security in the UK.

For such campaigns to change behaviour, the intended audience must be exposed to the message and pay attention to it. Poor or passive attention paid to information will undermine its effect (Parrott, 1995). Interest in and involvement with the subject matter is an important factor in maintaining 'active attention' and processing of the information.

Parrott (1995) suggests that to promote active processing:

- the presentation of the information should be unusual or unfamiliar;
- there should be a discrepancy between expectations of the information and the reality;
- the information should request the audience to do something, as this forces an increase in the level of attention.

There is also evidence that campaigns are more effective if they relate to subjects associated with strong public opinion and concern, and topics on which there is generally a consensus of opinion (O'Keefe *et al,* 1996).

The research reported here drew on some of these findings. The information formats were designed to be attention grabbing and many of the facts presented were known to be surprising. There is no doubt that there is a widespread negative consensus of views on sentencing in particular, and that interest in law and order issues tends to be quite high. In the initial survey 37 per cent of the public said they were very interested, and a further 53 per cent were fairly interested in law and order issues.[6]

What sort of information might have an influence on knowledge and attitudes?

This research compared three different information formats: printed material in the form of a booklet, a seminar event, and a video using footage of one of the seminars combined with other images.

Audio-visual and printed sources are most commonly described as the main source of information about crime and the criminal justice system. Three-quarters of people mention the television and radio news. Television documentaries, local and tabloid newspapers are mentioned by about half of respondents. Broad-sheet newspapers are an important source for about a third (Mirrlees-Black, 2001).

Some previous work using a technique called deliberative polling was filmed and made into a television programme by Channel 4. This suggested that face-to-face discussion was influential in changing attitudes about crime. However, critics suggest that some of this success may be due to demand characteristics. That is, where participants know what the research is trying to achieve they may consciously or unconsciously comply with this (Ladd, 1996). This may be a particular issue where the event is to be televised, as was recognised by the organisers.[7] This is a criticism that could also be levelled at the research reported here, although perhaps to a lesser extent as the research was not televised, and the purpose was not made explicit. Other criticisms directed at similar deliberative polling exercises in the US have included the questionnaire designs and the low response rates at follow-up stages (Kay, 1996).

In the US, members of the public from Alabama and Delaware were more likely to advocate alternatives to custody for non-violent offenders after seeing and discussing a video detailing the problem of prison overcrowding and alternative programmes. The information provided was specifically targeted at changing opinion on this particular issue (Doble, 1997; Doble and Immerwahr, 1997).

6. General population sample N = 1022.
7. Fishkin refers to this effect in describing the UK criminal justice deliberative poll, "Knowing that they would be on national television, they began discussing the topic with family and friends, they began to read newspapers and listen to the media with more care." Fishkin (1996).

There have been no previous attempts to evaluate the differential effects of alternative information formats on attitudes to criminal justice. Psychological research has found most support for the hypothesis that information in a printed form leads to better recall than that in audio or audio-visual formats. Furnham, Gunter and Green (1990) review the literature covering experiments that have used different types of information, including news and advertisements. They report that the finding holds even when the amount of time spent looking at or listening to the information is controlled for. It also holds whatever the mode of questioning (written or verbal).

Structure of the report

The development of the information sources and the methodology of the research are described in chapter 2. Chapter 3 discusses the improvements in knowledge found for the three information formats. Chapter 4 looks at beliefs about sentencing aims and practice. The impacts on attitudes and confidence in the system are described in chapter 5. Chapter 6 looks at the respondents' evaluation of the information formats. Chapter 7 draws together the findings and implications for policy in this area.

2 The information formats

A randomly selected sample of 1022 members of the general public answered a questionnaire about knowledge of crime and sentencing (see Appendix A). They were also asked a range of questions to assess their attitudes to the CJS and specifically to sentencing.[8] Some of those interviewed were asked to take part in the further stages of the research, and either received a booklet about crime and sentencing (109 people), attended a seminar (37 people), or watched a video (74 people).[9] Response rates for the different stages are discussed in chapter 4. Low take up was an issue, particularly for the seminar. This affects the 'representativeness' of each group and makes it more difficult to determine whether measured differences between the groups over the course of the research can be attributed to the relative impact of the information formats, rather than the initial profile of the groups.

All the information formats included the same key items of information. These included the correct answers to questions about crime and sentencing in the first stage questionnaire. The facts were drawn from sources most widely accepted as reliable, including recorded crime statistics, court proceeding statistics, and the British Crime Survey. After receiving the information, the participants were re-interviewed.[10] This design allowed an examination of changes in knowledge and attitudes, and the relationship between these, if any. It also allowed close control of the design of the information source materials and content. It was important that the source materials had similar content so that differences between them could be more confidently attributed to the format of the information, rather than differences in content.

8. The aim in the first stage was to obtain a representative sample of the general public aged 16 or over. The sample was clustered because of the need for seminar participants to be within a reasonable distance of the venue. Sampling points were selected systematically, stratified by region and social class. Respondents were selected randomly, using systematic selection of sampling points stratified by region and social class. Postcode sectors were then selected within the sampling points. The data were weighted to the population by region for analysis.
9. Quotas were used to ensure that the groups receiving the different information sources were well balanced. The participants received financial incentives to take part. Those in the seminar groups received £40, plus travelling expenses. Those who read the booklet or watched the video received £20 each.
10. The interviews were conducted by a research company using Computer Assisted Personal Interviewing where the questionnaire responses are entered directly on to a portable computer by the interviewer. See Appendix A for a copy of the questionnaire.

The booklet

The text of the booklet was designed to be simple and easy to understand, and was rather more geared to the general public than most Home Office research and statistics publications. Some charts and pictures were included. It was a square, CD size with 24 brightly coloured pages with a modern font. On many pages there were 'call-outs' where short parts of the text were reproduced and enlarged. The information was presented in the order of the criminal justice process: from crime levels, through policing to courts and sentences. A list of further contacts for information was included at the back. The booklet can be accessed at http://www.homeoffice.gov.uk/rds/horspubs1.html or copies can be obtained from the Communication Development Unit, RDS, at the Home Office.

The seminar

Four seminars were held, one in each of London, Manchester, Cardiff and Birmingham. Each started with a presentation by a senior academic. This covered the facts about crime and sentencing included in the text of the booklet. Visual aids were used where appropriate.[11] The seminar continued with presentations from a local prison governor and senior probation officer. These speakers detailed what an offender might experience in prison and under probation service supervision respectively. All the speakers based their presentations on a previously agreed script, to ensure reliability between the different sessions. Those attending were then divided into groups to discuss the issues raised, facilitated by researchers. They were asked to discuss the aims of sentencing, what they found surprising in the presentations, and if anything said had changed their views. The group then reconvened and questions were put to the academic expert and the prison and probation representatives. Each seminar lasted about three hours.

The video

The London seminar was filmed, and this formed the basis of a 37-minute video, together with footage of street scenes, police cars, courts, prisons and interviews with prisoners. A professional voice-over introduced the topic and linked sections together. Parts of the seminar question and answer session were also included.

11. In most cases this was using OHPs, but in London, which was filmed for the video, handouts were used but retrieved before the respondents left to avoid confusing the impact of the video and written material.

3 Improving knowledge

Knowledge of the criminal justice system was measured by 11 questions asked of the full 1022 sample and also in the follow-up questionnaire. Five of the questions asked about criminal justice processes and the other six covered statistical information about crime and sentencing. The format of questions varied from multiple choice to open response.

Table 3.1 lists the questions, the acceptable range of a correct answer, and the proportion of both the general population and the project participants who answered correctly. Also shown is the percentage that might be expected to get the question correct if answering by just guessing, i.e. by chance. The first column gives an indication of levels of knowledge amongst the general population. The second column shows that the 220 respondents who participated in the information project had a similar pattern of knowledge but initially scored slightly higher on most items.

Overall, knowledge of CJS processes and statistics is not good. The highest score achieved was eight out of 11, and that by just two of the 1022 sample. The mean score was 3.6. The expected average score if the questions had been answered entirely by guessing is 3.3. Fifteen people failed to get any questions correct.

There was considerable variation in the proportion of correct answers for different questions, but to some extent this reflects question format. For instance, although knowledge of justice processes appears relatively good, with around a half of people answering these questions correctly, their multiple choice format means there was between a 20 and 50 per cent probability of getting them correct through chance.

Knowledge of crime trends and current sentencing practice is particularly poor, with only about one in ten people being reasonably well informed in these areas. In line with previous research (e.g. Hough and Roberts, 1998) the use of custody for burglary is considerably under-estimated. Eight in ten respondents thought half or less of adult male burglars were given custodial sentences, although the actual proportion for 1999 was 72 per cent. Over a third of respondents thought the mandatory sentence for third time burglars was one year, and one in five thought it was three months. This perceived lenience of the system extends also to the length of custodial sentences with the vast majority of respondents under-estimating the length of a sentence for an adult male rapist. Two-thirds of respondents thought it would be five years or less, but in 1999 it averaged 8.5 years.

Table 3.1: Percentage of correct answers to the knowledge questions (a) that would be expected by chance (b) for the general population sample (GPS) (c) for the project participants

Question	Correct answer	Expected percent correct (due to chance)	Percent correct GPS n=1022	Percent correct Participants Before n = 220
In a magistrates' court a jury decides whether someone is guilty or not.	FALSE	50	64	71
In the Crown Court it is the jury who decide the sentence for an offender	FALSE	50	47	53
What is the minimum sentence for an adult who has been convicted three times of house burglary?	Three year prison sentence	25	28	33
Which is the most common sentence given by the courts for all offences (except motoring)?	Fine	25	50	54
Approximately how much of a prison sentence is spent in prison (not including life sentences)?	A half	25	47	50
Prisoners serving a 12-month or longer sentence will be supervised on release	TRUE	50	44	42
An offender is least likely to get convicted again if he is given a prison sentence, a community penalty, or does it makes no difference?	It makes no difference	33.3	45	48
Out of 100 convicted adult male burglars (21 and over) how many go to prison?	64 to 80	20	8	9
An adult male (21 and over) convicted of rape will get an average sentence length of?	8 to 9 years	12.5	6	8
Roughly how much does it cost to keep a prisoner in prison for a year?	£21k to £31k	17	11	10
What do you think has happened to the crime rate for the country as a whole over the past two years?	Less crime	20	8	11

Who knows most?

There was little systematic variation in how poorly informed people were, though men did slightly better than women and those under 65-years-old better than the over 65s.

Not surprisingly, those who have had contact with the criminal justice system have higher levels of overall knowledge, as do those who are more interested in law and order issues. People's own assessment of their knowledge level was correlated to their actual scores, but even those who described themselves as 'very knowledgeable' only had a mean score of 4.1.

Those with university level of education scored marginally higher, as did those in the AB socio-economic bracket. There is of course considerable overlap between these two groups. The statistical technique of logistic regression identifies those factors that are independently related to having a better level of knowledge, taking account of these overlaps. This indicates that contact with the CJS, being under 65 in age, of higher socio-economic class and not being 'very worried' about crime are all independently related to scoring above average.[12] Level of education and interest in the subject matter are not.

Changes in knowledge

The information required to answer all the questions correctly was given in the booklet, seminar and video, but even so, only one person got all 11 correct on the follow-up questionnaire. However, there was a significant increase in correct answers for each of the three groups (Figure 3.1). The video group showed the largest increase, with an average improvement of 2.5 questions. This could be a memory effect as, on average, the video group were re-interviewed within a shorter timeframe than those in the other two groups (see chapter 6).

12. The variables in Table 3.2 were used to model the likelihood of scoring four or more.

Table 3.2: Variations in mean knowledge score in the general population sample

		Mean score			Mean score
Male	16 to 34	3.7	Contact with CJS	Victim reporting crime	3.6
	35 to 64	3.9		In court for any reason	3.8
	65 +	3.5		In court as defendant	3.9
	All	3.7		In prison or YOI for any reason	4.0
Female	16 to 34	3.5	Attitudes to crime and CJS	Very interested	3.7
	35 to 64	3.5		Fairly interested	3.6
	65 +	3.2		Not interested	2.9
	All	3.4	How knowledgeable are you?	Very	4.1
Education	Higher	3.8		Fairly	3.7
	Further	3.6		Not very	3.5
	GCSE / trade	3.6		Not at all	3.0
	No qualifications	3.3	Worry about being the victim of crime	Very worried	3.3
Class	AB	3.8		Fairly worried	3.6
	C1	3.5		Not very worried	3.7
	C2	3.5		Not at all worried	3.5
	DE	3.5			
News source	Broad-sheet papers	3.6			
	Tabloids	3.6			
	Local papers	3.7			
	TV and radio	3.7	ALL		3.6

Source: General population sample: N=1022.

Figure 3.1: Change in mean knowledge score, by information source

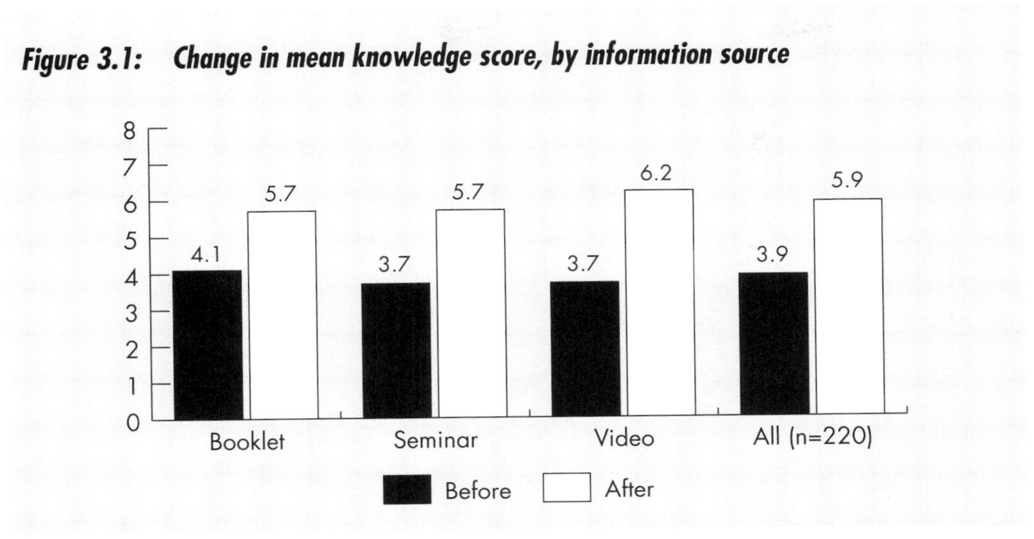

Some types of information seemed to have more of an impact than others. There were statistically significant increases in the proportion of people correctly answering questions about crime trends, prison place costs, sentence length, and supervision of longer-term prisoners on release (Table 3.3). There was less change in understanding of the role of the jury, where knowledge was initially relatively good, or in the relative effect of prison and community penalties on reconviction rates (the concept of 'no difference' apparently being difficult to take in).[13]

There is some evidence that the more 'surprising' the information, the more it is remembered. The annual cost of a prison place was frequently mentioned as surprising, and this was the question that showed the most dramatic improvement.

Further evidence of what makes information memorable can be construed where the booklet, video and seminar had a differential impact on increases in knowledge. For instance, only the booklet group were more likely to identify the fine as the most common sentence. This piece of information was given once in the video and (as far as we can tell) the seminar, but was repeated three times within the text of the booklet. Repetition appears to be effective then.

Only the seminar group showed much of an increase in knowledge about the proportion of a custodial sentence spent in prison. Transcripts of seminar discussions were not kept, but it may be that this was a point the presenters drew attention to, or was questioned by participants.

13. When asked if there were any parts they did not understand, some of the booklet group indicated that they had difficulty understanding the chart showing reconviction rates for community penalties and prison, because the trends were so similar. This chart has not been included in the revised version of the booklet.

Table 3.3: Overall percentage improvement in proportion answering the question correctly, by information source

	Booklet		Seminar		Video	
	Before	After	Before	After	Before	After
In a magistrates' court a jury decides whether someone is guilty or not.	71	77	78	87	68	81 *
In the Crown Court it is the jury who decide sentence for an offender.	58	57	57	68	43	55
What is the minimum sentence for an adult male burglar convicted three times for house burglary?	35	39	24	49 *	35	64 *
Which is the most common sentence given by the courts for all offences (except motoring)?	56	68 *	57	57	50	57
Approximately how much of a prison sentence is spent in prison (not including life sentences)?	55	61	51	81 *	43	50
Prisoners serving a 12-month or longer sentence will be supervised on release.	46	64 *	32	57 *	42	70 *
An offender is least likely to get convicted again if he is given a prison sentence or a community penalty?	51	55	41	46	46	45
Out of 100 convicted adult male burglars, how many go to prison?	11	26 *	11	14	5	28 *
An adult male (21 and over) convicted of rape will get an average sentence length of?	8	29 *	5	24 *	8	55 *
Roughly how much does it cost to keep a prisoner in prison for a year?	7	50 *	14	59 *	14	76 *
What has happened to the crime rate for the country over the past two years	13	39 *	3	30 *	12	41 *

Source: Participant sample. Booklet n = 109; Seminar = 37; Video = 74.
* = Statistically significant difference at the $p<0.05$ level. Other differences are not statistically significant.

Whose knowledge improved?

The largest increases in knowledge overall were amongst those who knew the least initially, while the lowest were amongst those who knew the most initially (Table 3.4). This was despite the fact that everyone had plenty of room for improvement, and could in principle have improved their scores by as much as the poorest knowledge group.

Women improved slightly more than men, the young more than the older age groups.

Again, generally speaking those with educational qualifications, and thus experience of learning (or scoring reasonably in exams at least) did best. The class variations will also reflect this to some extent, as perhaps do the greater gains amongst the broadsheet newspaper readership. Being interested in the topic didn't seem to help information retention, while worry about victimisation seems to act as a positive barrier.

Conclusion

Levels of knowledge are generally poor. This is widespread across all socio-demographic groups and it is hard to identify any particular group that would particularly benefit from a targeted information campaign. It is certainly important not to restrict information dissemination to those who have contact with the criminal justice system.

Substantial proportions of all groups thought they had learnt a lot from participating in the study. The seminar was rated most highly, with three-quarters saying they had learnt a lot, followed by the video group. In fact, increased knowledge of crime and sentencing, or at least recall of key facts, was achieved through all the information sources. The initial variations in the composition of the three groups make it difficult to identify any real differences between the formats in their effectiveness here. There were differences in the type of information that was taken on board. In some cases this was probably due to the way it was presented, but surprise is also clearly an important variable, with those facts that were thought particularly surprising most likely to be recalled. Some types of people were better at recalling the information they had been given. Perhaps not surprisingly, those with academic qualifications were the most adept at this. But the greatest gains were amongst those who scored lowest initially, whatever their level of education.

Table 3.4: Indexed change in mean knowledge score, with positive scores indicating an above average improvement, and negative scores a below average improvement

		Indexed			Indexed
Male	16 to 34	30	News source	Broadsheets	30
	35 to 64	-40		Tabloids	-20
	65 +	-10		Local papers	-10
	All	-20		TV and radio	-10
Female	16 to 34	50	Contact with CJS	Victim reporting crime	10
	35 to 64	10		In court for any reason	20
	65 +	-80		In court as defendant	-60
	All	10		In prison or YOI for any reason	-60
Education	Higher	40	Attitudes to crime and CJS	Very interested	-10
	Further	30		Fairly interested	-10
	GCSE / trade	0		Not interested	60
	No qualifications	-100	How knowledgeable are you?	Very or fairly	-30
Class	AB	50		Not very or not at all	20
	C1	0	Worry about being the victim of crime	Very worried	-70
	C2	-50		Fairly worried	-20
	DE	-40		Not very or not at all worried	30
Initial level of knowledge	2 or less correct	160			
	3 correct	40			
	4 correct	-10			
	5 correct	-80			
	6 or more correct	-120	ALL		0

Notes: Source participant sample n = 220.
Logistic regression indicates that all the characteristics shown are independently related to a change in knowledge level, except for news source and self-rated knowledge.

4 Beliefs about sentencing aims and practice

Public opinion about sentencing will, of course, be influenced by the purpose they assign it, and the extent to which current practice is perceived as delivering this. Beliefs about the purpose of sentencing were measured in the survey by questions asking generally about what the main aims of sentencing should be, and a task of ranking seven possible aims. A range of disposals were then assessed on how well they achieved these aims. A sentencing task was also completed for two types of offence and offender.

Main aim of sentencing

When asked unprompted what the main purpose of sentencing should be, the most frequent responses given were that it should stop re-offending, reduce crime, or create a safer community. Only around 20 per cent spontaneously mentioned punishment, and 11 per cent incapacitation. When asked to pick one of seven stated aims as the most important, 'changing the behaviour or attitudes of an offender to prevent them re-offending' was chosen most often.[14] A utilitarian belief in sentencing as a measure to reduce crime is widely held, whether realistic or not. It is likely that people believe reduced offending will be a consequence of 'tougher sentencing' and that this is in fact what 'punishment' is intended to achieve, rather than being an aim in itself. Doble (1997) found that people in Alabama felt the top priority for the criminal justice system was to protect people from becoming victims of crime, rather than any of the aims of sentencing such as deterrence, incapacitation or just deserts which professionals tend to think in terms of.

The purpose or aims of sentencing were not explicitly covered in the information formats. It was stated that the sentence of the court depends largely on the seriousness of the crime. Information was included on the effectiveness of disposals in reducing re-offending. There was no direct reference to 'just deserts'. The choice of aims after receiving information changed only slightly. The video group showed the biggest shift, away from changing behaviour, to punishment, but this change was not statistically significant (Table 4.1).

14. In the first stage, general public survey, 48 per cent of people chose this option.

Table 4.1: Percentage support for different 'main aims' of sentencing before and after receiving information

Main Aim of Sentencing	GPS	Booklet		Seminar		Video	
		Before	After	Before	After	Before	After
	%	%	%	%	%	%	%
Change behaviour/attitudes	47	50	53	46	46	53	43
Punish	19	20	20	16	19	14	26
Scare the offender	10	8	8	8	11	11	10
Restrict opportunities to re-offend	10	10	9	5	8	11	14
Deter others from committing the same crime	6	6	2	11	5	7	5
Make amends to the victim for harm done	5	4	5	14	8	5	3
Express society's disapproval	2	2	3	0	3	0	0

Source: General Public Sample (N=1022) and Participant Sample (N=220)

How effective is sentencing at reducing crime?

The public clearly believe, or want to believe, that sentencing has some impact on crime reduction and community safety. The extent to which this is realistic is probably fairly limited in practice (see Halliday 2001, Appendix 6 for a review of the evidence). Some might argue, therefore, that it is unwise to raise public expectations too far in this regard. On the other hand, improved confidence in the system does appear to be predicated on a belief that sentencing does have an impact on crime. Most people believe that the sentences given by the courts currently have an impact on crime, although for the majority this is only 'a little' impact (60%) rather than 'quite a lot' or 'a great deal' (31%). The greater the perceived impact, the more confidence that the system was effective at bringing offenders to justice.[15]

Impact of information

Despite the information they were given on levels of re-conviction, the proportion of participants thinking sentencing had 'quite a lot' or a 'great deal' of impact on crime increased from 31 per cent to 42 per cent. The booklet and video groups' views changed more than those of the seminar group (Figure 4.1). Only the increase for the booklet group is statistically significant.

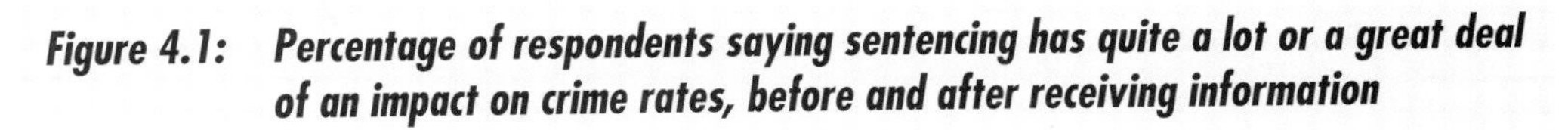

Figure 4.1: Percentage of respondents saying sentencing has quite a lot or a great deal of an impact on crime rates, before and after receiving information

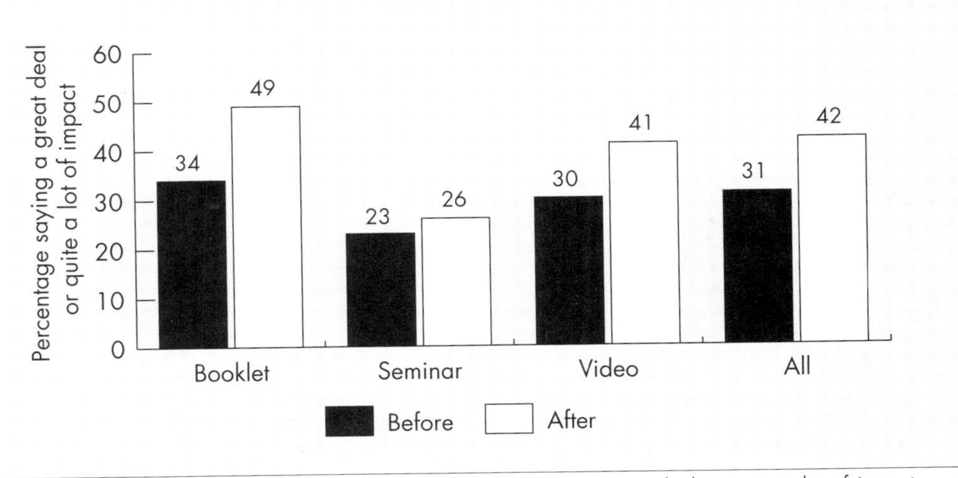

15. On the before survey, 51 per cent of those who thought it had a great deal or quite a lot of impact were confident the system was effective at bringing offenders to justice, compared to 38 per cent of those who thought it had a little impact, and 23 per cent of those who thought it had no impact.

How effective are specific sentences?

Different types of disposal varied considerably in the extent to which they were seen to be effective in reducing crime (Table 4.2).[16] Prison was thought to be the most effective in this respect, with 38 per cent of the general public thinking prison was 'very effective' at reducing crime, and a further 47 per cent thinking it was 'fairly effective'. A similar proportion thought prison combined with supervision in the community was effective, but the percentage thinking it was 'very effective' was lower.

The other established disposals, such as fines, probation orders and community service orders were less well rated – between 35 per cent and 49 per cent thought these disposals were very or fairly effective at reducing crime, but few of these thought they were 'very effective'.[17]

The concept of offenders compensating victims also received high ratings, an encouraging finding for restorative justice schemes and some of the recent youth justice reforms. The belief in drug treatment schemes no doubt reflects the finding that a third of the general public identify drugs as the main cause of crime (Mirrlees-Black 2001).

There is a considerable difference, then, between the way prison and other sentences are perceived in relation to crime reduction. This is not really surprising given its long history in the criminal justice system and as the pinnacle of the sentencing framework since the abolition of the death penalty. Nevertheless, many respondents also see the benefits of combining prison with supervision in the community. Some see this as preferable to a sentence just of imprisonment, even if the total length is the same: 72 per cent of the general public thought a sentence of three months custody followed by three months supervision would be more constructive than six months in prison.

Impact of information

After receiving information, participants tended to rate sentences as more effective at reducing crime (Table 4.2). However, for all disposals apart from prison and 'prison and supervision', the proportion saying they were *very* effective did not change much at all: the increases were in the proportion saying they were *fairly* effective. In contrast, for prison and 'prison and supervision' the percentage thinking they were *very* effective at reducing crime rose: for prison from 34 per cent to 43 per cent, and for 'prison and supervision' from 25 per cent to 33 per cent. There was little change in the proportion saying they were *fairly* effective, mainly because there were so few people thinking prison was not effective initially.

16. A sub-set of disposals were also rated in respect of some of the other aims of sentencing. See next section.
17. Probation Orders are now known as 'Community Rehabilitation Orders' and Community Service Orders as 'Community Punishment Orders'.

Table 4.2: Effectiveness of different sentences at reducing crime, before and after receiving information.

	General Public Survey		Participants before information		Participants after information	
	Very effective	Fairly effective	Very effective	Fairly effective	Very effective	Fairly effective
	%	%	%	%	%	%
Prison	38	47	34	49	43	48
Prison and supervision in the community	25	60	25	62	33	60
Offenders compensating and making amends	24	44	23	41	19	50
Drug Treatment Schemes	19	49	21	46	24	53
Electronic Tagging	10	45	7	48	5	46
Fines	5	38	5	37	4	44
Probation Orders	4	45	4	40	2	59
Community Service Orders	4	36	2	35	3	43

Source: General Public Sample, N=1022 and Participant sample (includes only those who answered the question both before and after) Minimum N=173

Table 4.3: Percentage of people thinking different sentences very or fairly likely to meet different aims of sentencing for a burglar and a robber.

	Change behaviour/attitudes		Punish		Restrict opportunities to re-offend		Deter others		Make amends to the victim	
	burglar	robber	burglar	robber	burglar	robber	burglar	robber	burglar	robber
	%	%	%	%	%	%	%	%	%	%
Imprisonment	74	79	78	85	87	87	77	81	71	76
Electronic tagging	53	46	54	45	74	69	47	43	25	21
Community Service	48	34	55	45	40	32	44	38	42	35

Source: General Public Sample (N=1022). Respondents were asked to rate each of the three sentences as 'very likely', 'fairly likely', 'not very likely' or 'not at all likely' to meet each aim.

How well do sentences serve other aims?

One criticism of asking the public to state their preferred aim of sentencing is that this is likely to vary according to the nature of the offence and the offender. To address this, the surveys included details of two offenders and offences. The first was John, a burglar, the second, Mike, a robber. Respondents were first asked to select an appropriate sentence assuming that John or Mike were first-time adult offenders, with multiple choice allowed. This exercise was then repeated on the assumption that they were now repeat offenders. They were then asked how likely they thought it was that each of prison, a community service order and electronic tagging, would meet different aims of sentencing for this particular offender (as a recidivist).[18]

The belief in prison as an effective method for reducing crime is also seen here. Prison was judged as very likely to punish, deter others, make amends to the victim, restrict re-offending and change behaviour, much more so than community service or electronic tagging.

Support for electronic tagging and community service is around 40 to 50 per cent as a method of punishing, deterring others and changing behaviour in the case of burglary, and generally slightly lower for robbery (Table 4.3). Neither type of disposal was seen as effective in making amends to the victim, particularly electronic tagging, with only 25 per cent believing tagging could achieve this in the case of the burglar. Tagging receives particularly high ratings, though, as a method of restricting offenders' opportunities to re-offend: 74 per cent thought it would be effective in this respect for a burglar and 69 per cent for a robber.

Impact of information

As the sample was split for these questions, the small numbers involved in some of the information groups are too small to look at change in response on these questions after receiving information.

Circumstances affecting sentencing

When considering factors to be taken into account when sentencing other than offence type or seriousness, the public felt that previous convictions and the likelihood of re-offending were very important: 99 per cent thought previous convictions should have some influence, with 86 per cent saying it should have a great deal of influence.

18. Although it wasn't explicitly stated that the offender was a recidivist, the questions followed on from this scenario.

Other factors to do with the offence and offending were also thought to be important. 54 per cent of respondents thought a great deal of notice should be taken of the effect of the crime on the victim, although the number thinking a great deal of notice should be taken of the wishes of the victim was lower (25%).

Personal circumstances, such as domestic responsibilities, age and employment status were not generally felt to be as important. Only 20 per cent thought a great deal of notice should be taken of domestic responsibilities.

Figure 4.2: Factors that should have a great deal or some influence on a sentence (General Public Sample N=1022)[19]

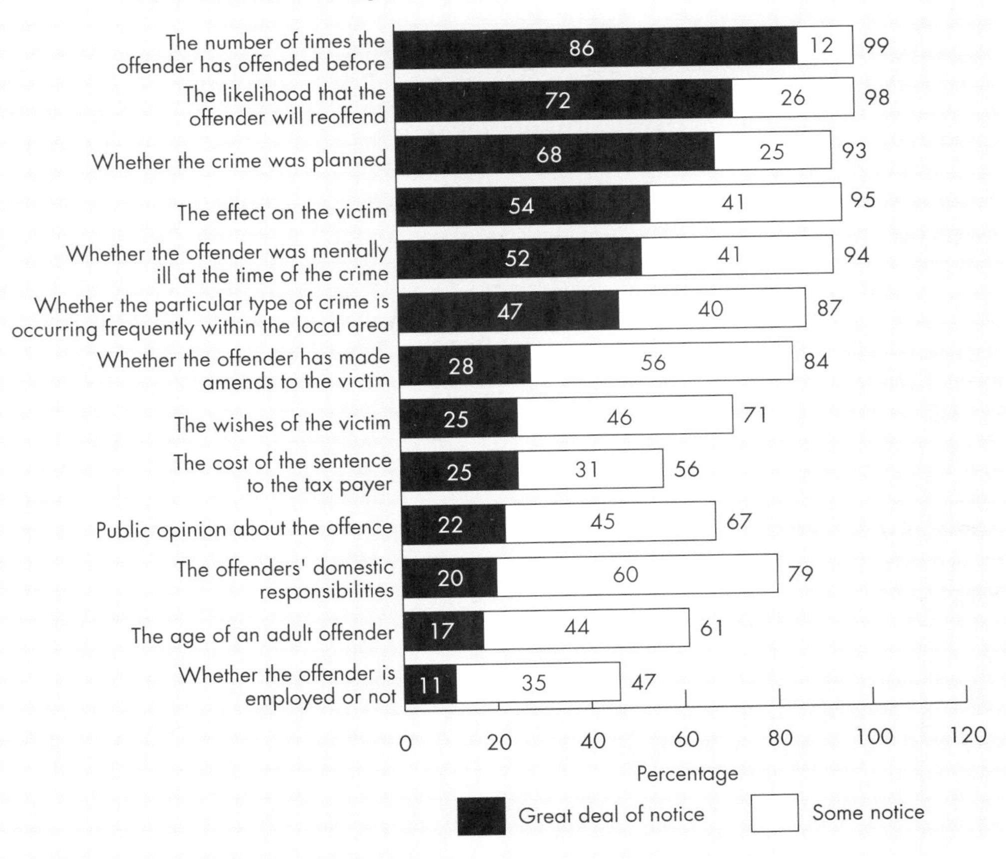

19. The individual values for a great deal and some influence may not add to the total given due to rounding.

Impact of information

For the booklet and seminar groups, there were no significant changes in the importance respondents attached to these factors. After seeing the video, this group were more likely to think that the likelihood of re-offending, the number of times the offender has offended before and the age of the offender should be taken into account in sentencing. However they were less likely to think that sentencing should take notice of the wishes of the victim.

Sentencing practice in specific cases

Despite the confidence in prison to meet a wide range of sentencing aims, there was evidence that people would rather reserve it for those they consider to be the most serious criminals. When sentencing the two offenders in the scenarios as first-time offenders, use of prison was very low.[20] John the burglar was given prison as part of his sentence by only 9 per cent of respondents. 21 per cent of people said they would have sent Mike the robber to prison. Even when they became repeat offenders, only 56 per cent opted to give John a prison sentence, although 74 per cent now felt this was appropriate for Mike.[21] The rates of use of custody are much lower than would be received by offenders committing these sorts of crimes.[22]

Other than the financial cost of prison – a fact that many participants expressed surprise at – other costs are also recognised. There is awareness, for instance, of the potentially damaging effects of prison, and this may partly explain the restraint in the use of prison shown above. Two-thirds (68%) of the general public strongly or moderately agreed that 'offenders come out of prison worse than they go in'. It may be that when answering this question, they are reminded of the common perception that prison is a 'university of crime' but it could also be that they are expressing concern about perceived easy conditions or regimes in prisons.

Impact of information

Certainly the effect of giving participants information about prison regimes was an improvement in confidence in the efficacy of prison. The proportion agreeing that 'offenders come out of prison worse than they go in' fell from 72 per cent to 59 per cent. Participants

20. Respondents were not required to recall what sentences were available; rather they were asked, for each sentence, whether they would use it for the offender. These questions followed other discussions about which sentences respondents were aware of, both unprompted and prompted, so by this stage of the interview they had some familiarity with the sentences available.
21. Findings from General Public Survey of 1022 people.
22. 75 per cent of burglars are given custodial sentences, as are 91 per cent of those convicted of robbery.

generally became more supportive and understanding of prison procedures. For instance, they were more likely to agree that there is a need for incentives for good behaviour and that prisoners need support in preparing them for release.

As far as the choice of sentences was concerned, the use of prison for John and Mike remained about the same (Figure 4.3).[23] There were also few changes in the use of other sentences. Fines were used a little more often for the burglar. Previous research such as Hough and Roberts (1999) and Doble (1997) has found that increasing information about the availability of alternatives leads to a greater use of alternatives to custody. Given that in the current research participants sentencing preferences were already more lenient, if anything, than judicial practice, and that the respondents had already been reminded of available sentences, this lack of change is not surprising.

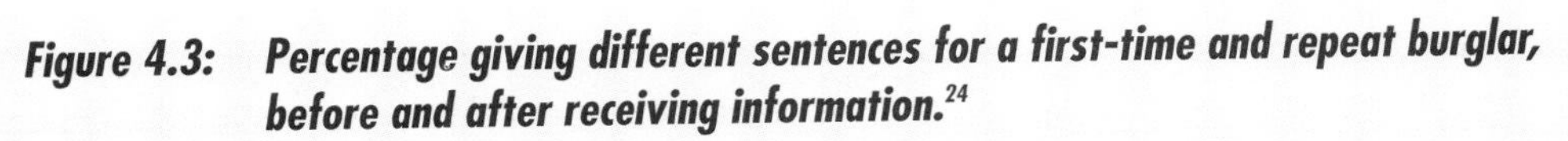

Figure 4.3: Percentage giving different sentences for a first-time and repeat burglar, before and after receiving information.[24]

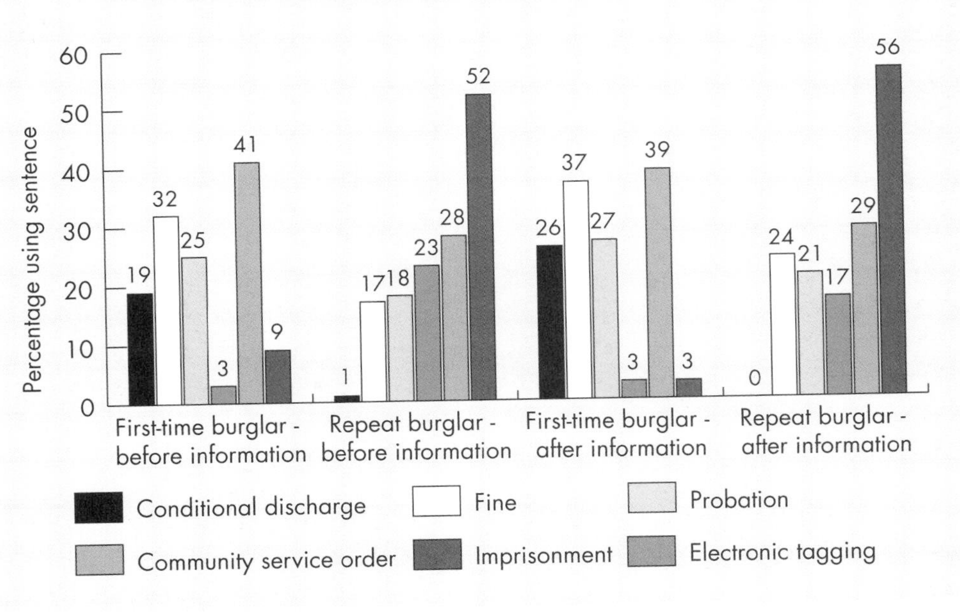

23. The patterns of use of sentences for those taking part in the second stage, before receiving information, are very similar to those reported above for the general public survey.
24. Participants could choose as many different sentences in combination as they wanted. This included conditional discharge and some participants chose this as well as other sentences. Therefore the number shown here choosing conditional discharge should not be interpreted as the number giving this and no other penalty.

Conclusion

Receiving information did not change participants' views about sentencing aims and practices very much. Crime reduction and changing behaviour were identified as the most important aims of sentencing both before and after receiving information.

Prison was widely believed to be effective at reducing crime and in achieving other aims of sentencing. Receiving information led to an increase in support for alternatives, but also to a greater increase in support for prison.

Use of custody by respondents in particular cases was considerably lower than the rates given by the courts for these types of cases. Providing information did not change this.

5 Changes in attitudes and confidence

This chapter evaluates the effect of the booklet, seminar and video on three key attitude measures: worry about victimisation, perceived lenience of sentencing, and confidence in the criminal justice system. For each of the measures, the characteristics of those people who were more likely to change their opinions are identified. As discussed in chapter 1, the known relationship between levels of knowledge about crime and the CJS and attitudes to the CJS suggested that giving people information would have a positive impact on their attitudes. This chapter considers the extent to which changes in attitude can be attributed to improved levels of knowledge.

Worry about victimisation

Worry about victimisation has been associated with poor knowledge, particularly in regard to crime trends and risks of victimisation. All of the information formats included a statement that according to police and BCS figures, there were now fewer crimes than in the early nineties. Each source also gave the relative risks of being attacked by strangers for people of different ages and gender. This showed the low risk to the elderly and women in comparison with young men.

Overall effects on worry about being a victim

Overall, there was a net reduction in worry amongst participants. This effect was mixed, though. Nearly a quarter of people reported reduced worry, but 15 per cent had an increased level of worry about becoming a victim. 38 per cent of the seminar group reported reduced worry, more than for the other information format groups (Figure 5.1).

Figure 5.1: Change in worry about being a victim by information format for those answering the question both before and after

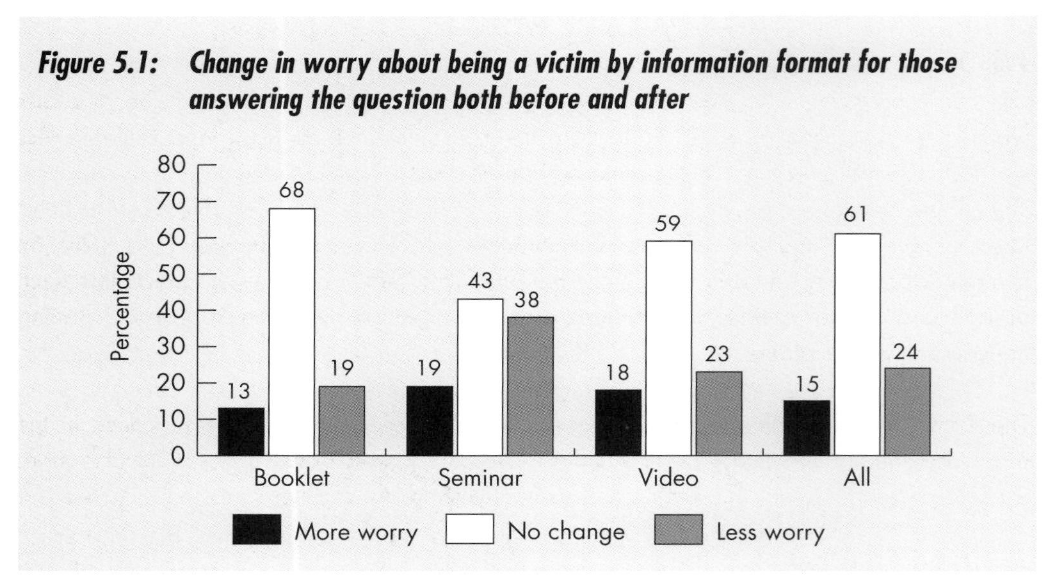

Initial level of worry was highly related to the likelihood of becoming less worried: 54 per cent of those who were initially 'very' worried became less worried, compared with 28 per cent of those who were 'fairly' worried and 9 per cent of those who were 'not very' worried. (Figure 5.2). Although over two-thirds of those who were 'not at all worried' before receiving information increased their level of worry, this was only slightly, to 'not very worried', and there were only seven people in this group.

Figure 5.2: Change in worry about being a victim by original level of worry.

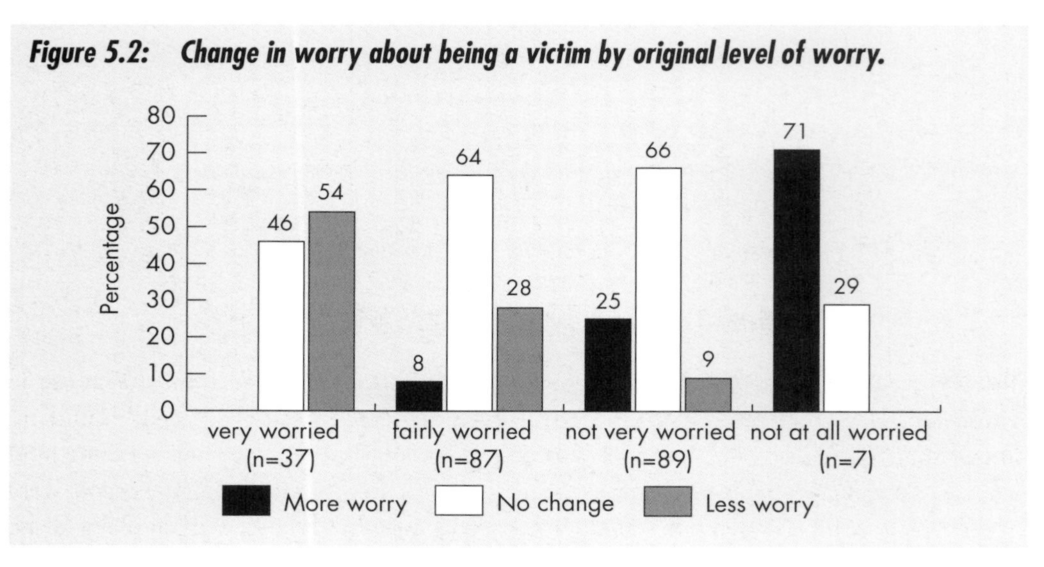

Who becomes less worried?

Of course the seven who initially said they were 'not at all worried' couldn't become less worried on the measure used. To explore the characteristics of those who became less worried these people were therefore excluded from the analysis.

Logistic regression analysis confirms that initial level of worry is associated with a reduction in worry about being a victim of crime, even when the impact of other characteristics, such as age and sex are held constant. Also associated with a reduction in worry is having educational qualifications.

The format in which information was received did not reach statistical significance in the regression model. Those who were very interested in law and order issues were also more likely to get less worried, but again this was not independent of other factors.

Knowledge and fear

Figure 5.3: Change in worry about being a victim of crime by change in knowledge

Percentage	More worry	No change	Less worry
worse or no change	18	60	22
one or two more correct	16	54	29
three more correct	9	72	19
4+ more correct	15	63	22

There was no evidence that an increase in knowledge was associated with a decrease in worry about victimisation (Figure 5.3). The logistic regression analysis found no independent effect of an increase in knowledge on worry. The 'very worried' were the most likely to become less worried but as shown in chapter 3, the initially very worried were among those who showed least improvement in knowledge scores. Participating in the project does seem to have had a positive effect on levels of worry, but it is not possible to identify why this is. It could, perhaps, be the experience of being involved in the project or an improved awareness of crime and the CJS that the questionnaires failed to detect.

Is sentencing too lenient?

The question 'in general would you say the sentences handed down by the courts are too tough, about right or too lenient?' has been used as an indicator of punitiveness, but is also useful as a barometer of how appropriate sentencing is seen to be, in comparison with expectations.

Overall effects on views of sentencing

The proportion thinking sentencing was about right increased from 21 per cent before receiving information to 31 per cent afterwards. The increase was largest for the booklet group. Very few people (3%) thought sentencing was too tough, either before or after receiving information.

Overall, over a quarter of participants became less punitive after receiving information (Table 5.1). The proportion for the booklet is a little higher than those for the seminar and video groups, but the difference between the groups is not statistically significant.

Table 5.1: Change in punitiveness after receiving information

	Booklet %	Seminar %	Video %	All %
More punitive	14	23	17	17
No change	55	51	58	55
Less punitive	31	26	26	28
N=	*105*	*35*	*66*	*206*

Looking just at those who answered the question both before and after receiving information, those who thought sentencing was much too lenient before receiving information were more likely to change their opinion and become less punitive than those who thought it was a little too lenient (Figure 5.4). About a third of those who thought sentencing was 'about right' before became more punitive. However, for all but one this was only a change to 'a little too lenient'.

Figure 5.4: Change in opinion about sentencing of the courts, by original opinion.

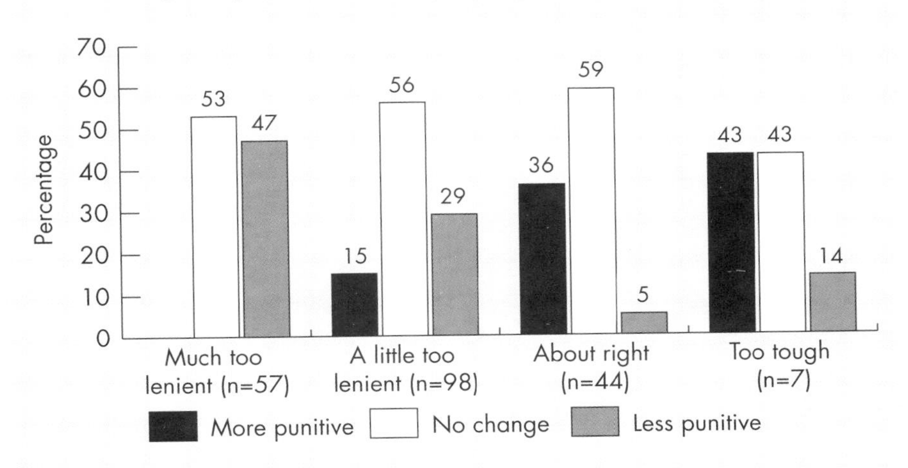

Participants who changed their opinion were asked why this was.[25] The answers included many explicit references to the information sources and how these had raised their awareness. There were also specific mentions of sentence lengths and the percentages of offenders given custodial sentences. The formats presented this information as three 'case studies' of offenders, their offences and the sentence they would expect to receive – both their likelihood of imprisonment and the average sentence for that offence.[26] One of the participants from the video group said: 'they were much tougher than I thought'. One of the booklet group said they had now given more thought to the question.

But not all those who had changed their opinion credited this to the information sources. Some made reference to the news, saying they had seen particular cases which had changed their views. Some participants thought the actual levels of sentencing had improved since the first interview. Others cited personal experience, either as a victim, or as an offender, or knowing an offender. Nevertheless there was some evidence of an indirect influence, as some felt taking part in the research had affected the way they approached the issues: 'I've been reading and my general impression now is it's about right' and 'Because I have been thinking more deeply about the problem since the first interview'.

25. Second stage interviews were matched in the CAPI program to some responses from the first stage. If the interviewee gave a different answer, they were asked: 'you said x before, why has your opinion changed?'.
26. The case studies involved John, who was a burglar, Mike who committed a robbery, and Frank who was a rapist.

Factors influencing views of sentencing

To identify the factors related to shifts in opinion towards believing sentencing practice is 'about right' logistic regression analysis was used, including just the 72 per cent (N=159) of participants who initially said sentences were 'a little' or 'much' too lenient. The small minority who initially thought it was 'too tough' were excluded as different factors are likely to be relevant for this group. The regression identified initial strength of belief, having educational qualifications, and improvement in knowledge after receiving information as independently predictive of shifts in opinion.

Effects of knowledge

Looking more specifically at responses of 'about right' before and after receiving information confirms that increased knowledge does seem to be a relevant factor (Figure 5.5). The proportion saying sentencing was 'about right' increased overall, but those improving their knowledge by one or two correct answers, or by four or more, showed the greatest increase.

Figure 5.5: Percentage saying sentencing 'about right', before and after receiving information, by change in knowledge

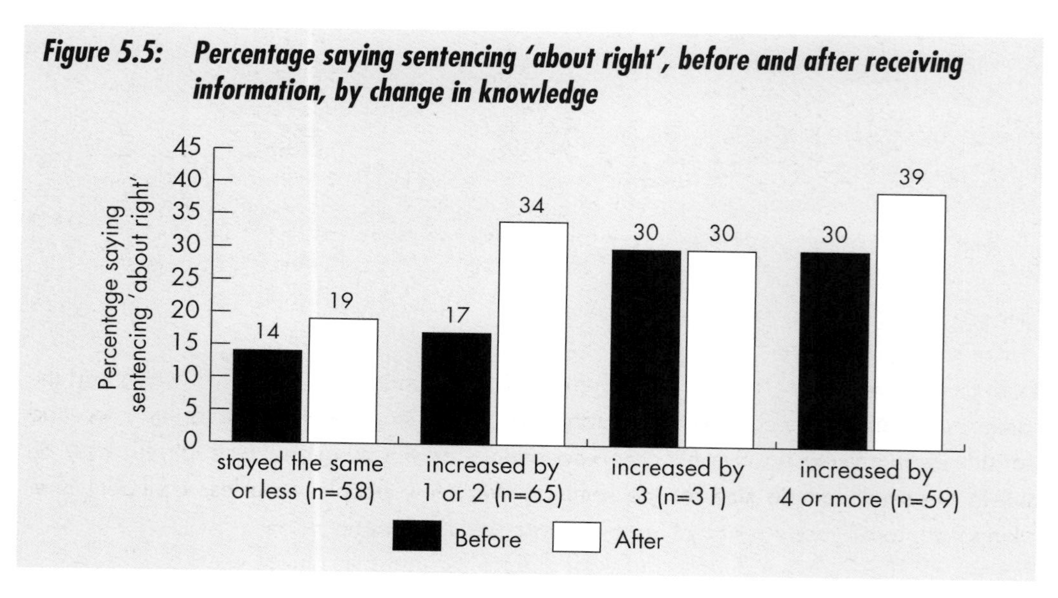

Confidence in the CJS

Overall changes in confidence

There were improvements in confidence for all three of the confidence indicators but that for confidence that the CJS meets the needs of victims did not reach statistical significance.[27] The greatest gains were in the number of participants who were confident that the CJS brings people who commit crimes to justice which increased after receiving information, from 38 per cent to 60 per cent (Figure 5.6).[28]

Figure 5.6: Percentage very or fairly confident in different aspects of the CJS, before and after receiving information

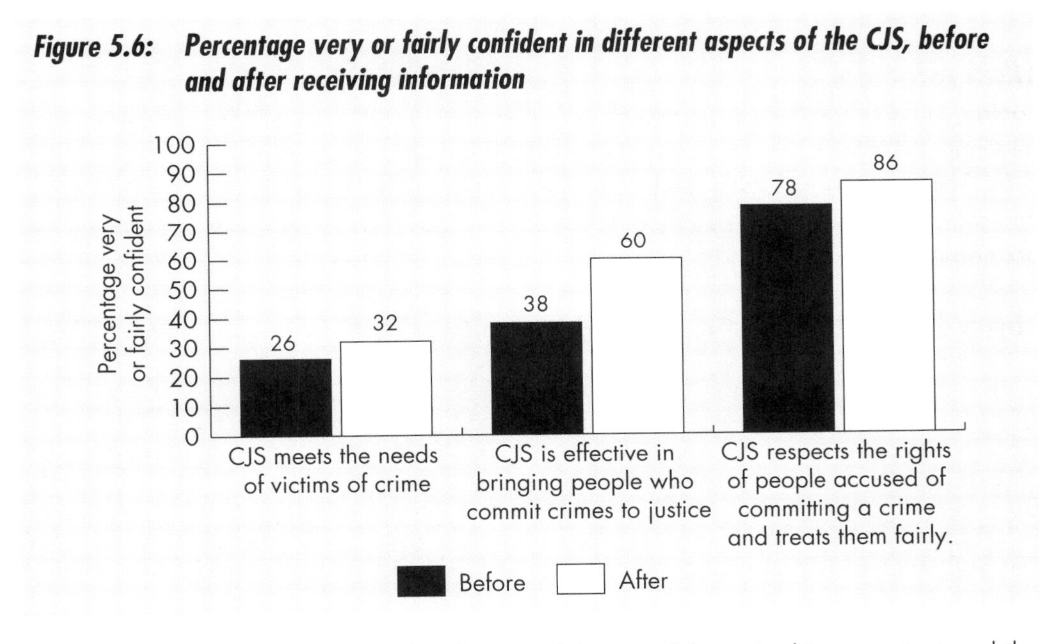

Figure 5.7 shows the proportion who decreased their confidence in this respect, stayed the same, or became more confident, by information type. Only the booklet and the video had statistically significant positive effects on confidence on this measure (although this may be due to the small sample size for the seminar). Very few people were less confident after taking part, and in each group at least 30 per cent were more confident.

27. Comparisons for those who answered the questions both before and after receiving information.
28. The fourth aspect of the CJS confidence is measured on as part of the CJS objective, 'deals with cases promptly and efficiently' was not included in the survey due to lack of space.

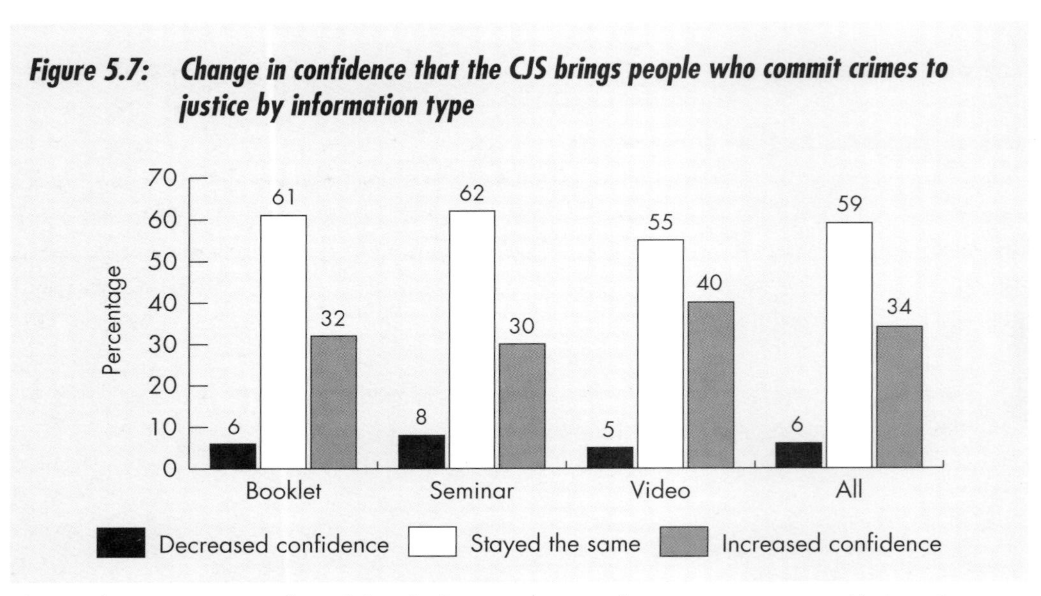

Those who were not at all confident before receiving information were most likely to become more confident that the criminal justice system brings people who commit crimes to justice (Figure 5.8).

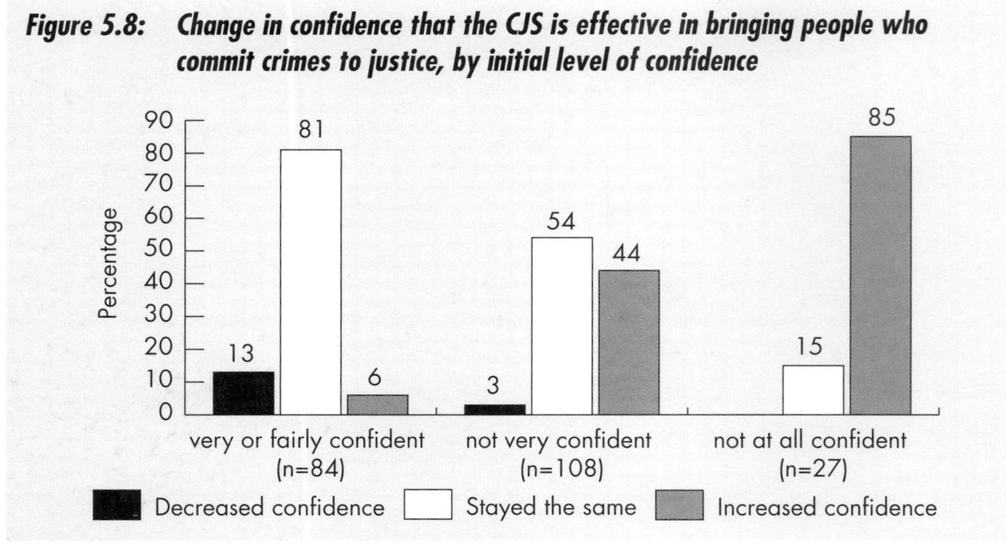

Factors related to becoming more confident

Improvement in confidence on this measure could only occur for the 98 per cent (N=216) who were not 'very confident' in the first stage survey. Logistic regression analysis shows that interest in law and order and original level of confidence are independently associated with change in confidence. Those who said they were very interested in law and order were less likely to improve in confidence. Those who were not at all confident were the most likely to improve in confidence.

Knowledge and confidence

Although participation in the project clearly had some impact on public confidence, there was no clear relationship between improved scores on the knowledge questions and improved levels of confidence (Figure 5.9).

Figure 5.9: Change in confidence that the CJS is effective in bringing people who commit crimes to justice, by change in knowledge

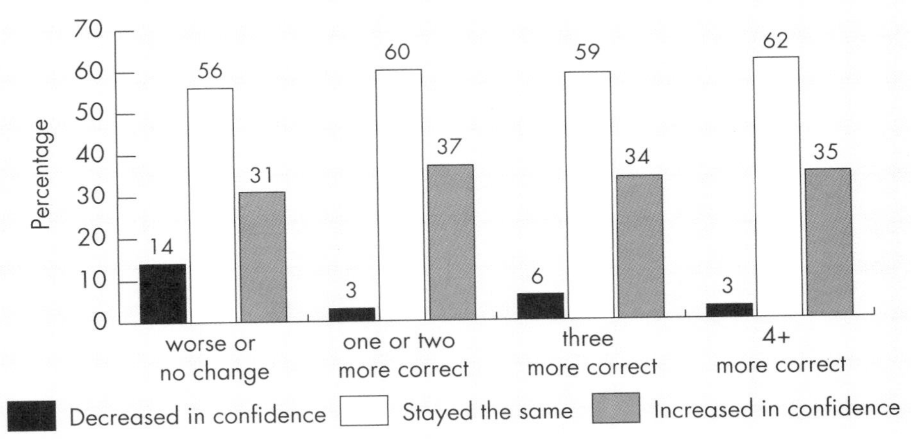

Conclusion

The small sample sizes involved make detailed analysis of patterns of change in attitudes and confidence difficult. However, it is possible to say that the information sources did have positive effects on fear of crime, on perceptions of sentencing practice, and in confidence that the criminal justice system brings people who commit crimes to justice.

There seems to be little systematic variation in improved attitudes according to socio-demographic characteristics. For all three attitudes, the most predictive factor is original level of attitude: those with the most extreme attitudes are most likely to change their opinions. Interest in law and order issues and levels of educational qualification also seem to be related to change in some of the attitudes. Who is susceptible to changing attitudes when presented with information may be partly dependent on other factors which were not measured, such as learning style.

Of these three attitude measures, improved knowledge scores were only found to be related to changes in judgements about the appropriateness of sentencing practice. However, the changes in fear and confidence may also have been brought about by the act of being given information, but not so directly related to improved recall of specific facts.

6 Evaluation of the information formats

Chapter 3 discussed the effectiveness of the three information formats in improving knowledge and chapters 4 and 5 their impact on attitudes. This chapter considers the extent to which each of the formats successfully reached its target audience, and how well they were received by those that read, attended or watched them.

Who took part?

Although every effort was made to ensure representative samples were offered each information type, there were some considerable differences in rates of participation. There were two main points at which people had the opportunity not to participate: the first when they were asked to take part in the second stage of the research, and the second at the actual point of participation. Reinterview could also 'lose' participants, either because they refused (which might be associated with not having looked at the information), or because there was not enough time to contact them. The video group, for whom the window for reinterview was shortest, lost the most participants at this final stage.[29]

This section looks at the change in participation rates between being asked to take part, and being reinterviewed at the second survey stage. There are limitations to this, including that it does not allow identification of loss of participants due to other circumstances, such as the time available for reinterview, as discussed above. It also does not show any differences that occurred at the initial selection stage (such as who refused to be interviewed in the first survey).

29. The time between receiving the information and the follow-up interview was one to two weeks for the video group, compared with between two and six weeks for the booklet group and one and six weeks for the seminar group.

Figure 6.1: Participation at different stages for the different information formats

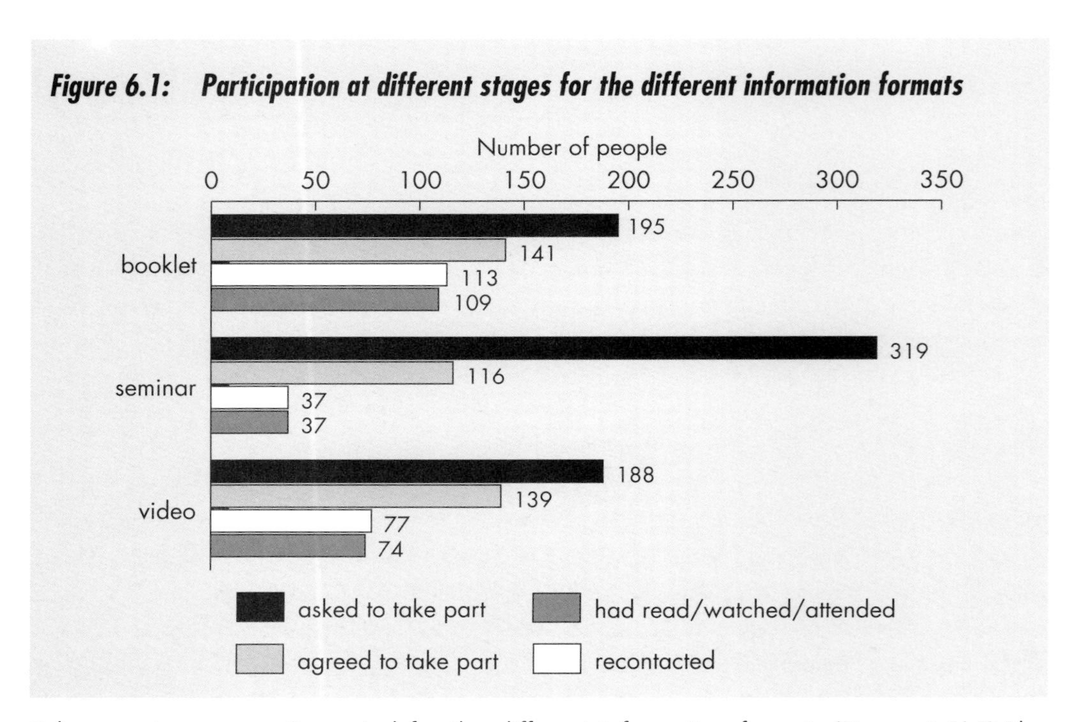

Take-up rates were quite varied for the different information formats (Figure 6.1).[30] The booklet had an agreement rate of 72 per cent, and a recontact rate of 80 per cent. The initial agreement rate for the seminar was much lower at 36 per cent, as was the percentage recontacted at 32 per cent (this is mainly due to the low numbers attending the sessions, rather than problems with recontact. Thirty-eight people attended the seminars and 37 were reinterviewed).[31] The video group had a reasonably good agreement rate of 74 per cent, but only 55 per cent of these were then recontacted. This is a particularly low rate, perhaps because the video was the last intervention to take place and the period available for reinterview was therefore the shortest. Low take-up rates, particularly for the seminar, affect the 'representativeness' of each group. This makes it difficult to determine whether the differences in outcomes between the groups are due to the impact of each information format, or the different make-up of the groups.

Table 6.1 shows the percentages of those who were asked to take part who were reinterviewed, by demographic group, for each information type.

30. Table C4.1 in Appendix C shows the take up and participation rates in more detail.
31. Because the number in this group is quite small, this makes it less likely that changes in variables reach statistical significance. It should be borne in mind, therefore, that more statistically significant changes may have been found with a larger group.

Table 6.1: Variations in participation in the information stage of the research – percentage of those asked to take part who were reinterviewed, by demographic group

	% of those asked in each demographic group who participated		
	Booklet	Seminar	Video
Sex			
Male	61	12	40
Female	56	11	42
Age			
16-34	66	10	40
35-64	60	14	41
65+	38	8	43
Ethnicity			
White	60	13	44
Non-white	25*	4	0*
Class			
AB	66	19	38
C1	52	12	38
C2	54	9	47
DE	58	9	43
Children in household			
Yes	67	12	41
No	54	12	41
Qualifications			
Degree or higher	60	18	40
A levels or diploma	52	11	31
GCSE or trade	68	14	48
Other or none	48	6*	41
Interest in law and order			
Very interested	56	16*	40
Fairly interested or not interested	59	9	42

	% of those asked in each demographic group who participated		
	Booklet	Seminar	Video
Think sentencing is			
Much too lenient	49	10	44
Little too lenient or less	62	15	40
Contact with the CJS			
Victim of crime	64	7	46
Not a victim	51	14	33
Been in court	57	10	46
Not been in court	58	15	38
Been in court as accused	80*	11	56
Not in court as accused	55	17	40
Been in a prison	72	11	57
Not been in a prison	56	14	39
News source			
Broadsheet	60	20*	30*
Not broadsheet	57	6	47
Tabloid	61	6*	42
Not tabloid	55	16	41
local paper	63	9	42
Not local paper	49	14	41
TV news	61	11	41
Not tv news	46	12	43
Has access to internet	65*	15	43
No access to internet	50	8	39
Knowledge about the CJS			
2 or less correct	38	5	29
3 or more correct	63*	14	45*
All	58	12	41

* Rate of participation significantly different than rate for other demographic groups at $p<0.05$ level

Two effects can be seen across all three of the information formats. Those from minority ethnic communities are less likely to take part, as are those with lower levels of existing knowledge.[32] The lower rates of participation for those from minority ethnic communities reflect findings from other research. For example, the British Crime Survey 2000 had a response rate for these groups of 58 per cent, compared with 74 per cent for whites. Lower participation rates from those with lower existing knowledge is disappointing, if this means that those who could most benefit from information do not receive it.

There were also some effects for the particular information formats. For the booklet, those more likely to take part were those:

- who have access to the internet; or
- who had previously been in court accused of a crime.

Of the people asked to take part in the seminar exercise, those who:

- had read a broadsheet newspaper in the last week or are very interested in law and order issues were more likely to take part;
- had read a tabloid in the past week were less likely to take part.

Of those asked to watch the video, those who had:

- read a broadsheet newspaper in the past week were less likely to take part.

When asked why they would not be willing to take part, the largest number of people said they were too busy, did not have enough time or cited other commitments. Others said they were just not interested. Being away on holiday or moving out of the area were other common reasons given for not taking part in the next stage. Some respondents said they thought they were too old. Others said they thought they had made enough of a contribution, or that the questionnaire was very long. A few said it was a waste of time as they thought their views would not change anything.

Those who took part were told they would be given financial incentives which they would receive after they were reinterviewed. It is likely that considerably fewer would have agreed to take part if there was no financial incentive. Future work planned will involve giving the booklet, with little explanation, to British Crime Survey respondents after their interview. They will be recontacted by 'phone to find out how many read it without the motivation of a financial incentive or an awareness that they were to be reinterviewed about it.

32. These results are not significant for the seminar group – it is likely this is a result of the small sample size for this group.

Discussion of the information with others

The participants in the booklet group were asked in the follow-up interview what they had done with the booklet after reading it. Only three people in the booklet group said they had thrown it away and a further three had given the booklet to a friend, although it is likely that respondents were keeping it until after the follow-up interview.

What respondents did with the materials and whether they discussed it with others may give an indication of how interesting they found it. Discussing the information with others is also an important method for further dissemination of the information, important for the effectiveness of any information campaign.

Those aged 16 to 24 and over 65 were more likely to have discussed the information with others than those in the other age groups. Also, those who had read a broadsheet newspaper in the last week were more likely to have discussed the information with someone else.

Of the information groups, the seminar participants discussed the information the most. Only one person did not discuss the seminar with anyone else, and 84 per cent discussed it with friends. Fewer people discussed the booklet and video. 61 per cent of the video group did not discuss it with others, and 43 per cent of the booklet group did not talk to other people about it (Figure 6.2). However, this leaves a large number of participants who did discuss the information with other people – a majority for the booklet and seminar groups.

Figure 6.2: Discussion of the information formats with others

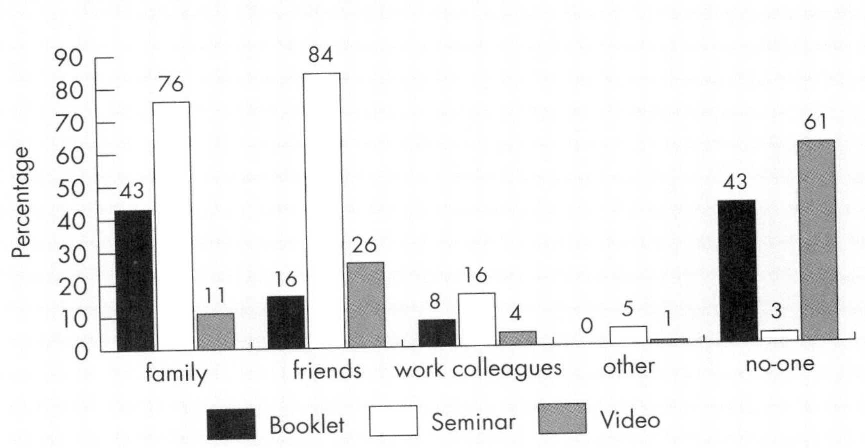

Ease of understanding, general impressions, usefulness and enjoyment

Although the information formats were carefully designed to be straightforward and easy to understand, inevitably some of the information presented was fairly complex. It is therefore reassuring that the majority of participants in all groups found the information very or quite easy to understand (Table 6.2). The seminar was thought to be slightly easier to understand than the booklet or video. This is not particularly surprising as those who attended the seminars had the opportunity to ask questions and clarify any points that were not clear at the time.

Table 6.2: Participant ratings of how easy the information sources were to understand.

	Booklet %	Seminar %	Video %
Very easy	62	73	57
Quite easy	35	27	43
Quite difficult	3	0	0
Very difficult	0	0	0
N	*109*	*74*	*37*

Participants were asked to rate the information sources on a number of dimensions. The mean rating (from 1 to 5) is shown in Figure 6.3. The higher the mean, the more positive the rating. All three information sources were rated as very easy to understand and informative. They were also all judged as reasonably interesting and helpful. The only dimension on which any of the average ratings were on the 'negative' side of the scale was the exciting/dull dimension – the video group having a mean ranking of 2.54 and the booklet 2.86. This is not really surprising as the information and subject matter is not particularly exciting – it is factual and for the most part relates to processes. The more positive ratings for ease of understanding and interesting/boring support this.

Figure 6.3: Mean ratings of the three information formats on various dimensions

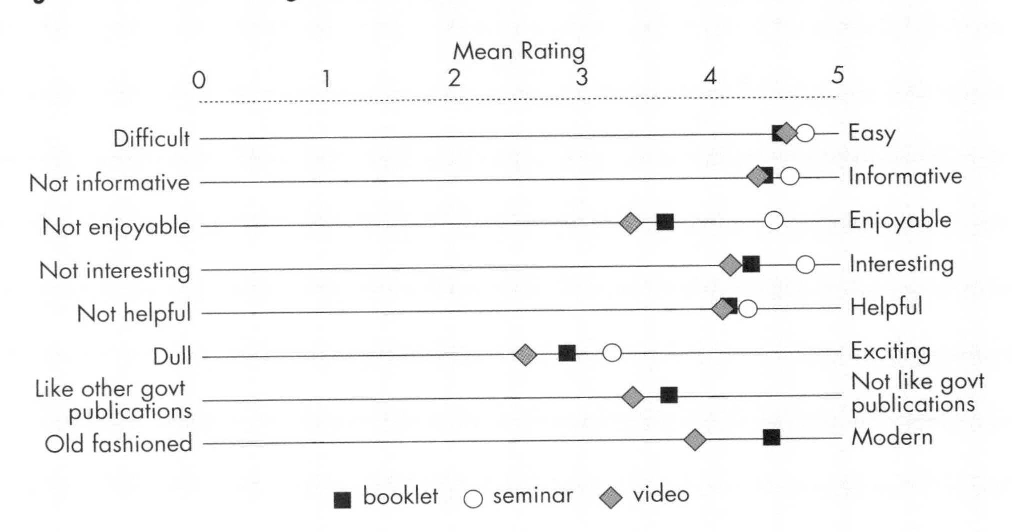

The seminar scored more positively than the other information sources on most dimensions, in some cases significantly so. For example, the seminar was seen as more enjoyable, interesting and exciting than the other information types. Two dimensions were only asked of the booklet and video participants. These were about perceptions of style and tone. Both the booklet and the video were rated positively – as being modern, and not like other government publications. The booklet was rated more positively than the video on both these dimensions.

Interesting topics

All three formats were rated as interesting by a majority of participants. The type of format had an impact on the extent to which the various topics covered were thought to be interesting. When asked which parts they found particularly interesting, the differences between the formats was more noticeable than the difference between subject areas (Figure 6.4). The seminar group rated all topic areas as more interesting than the video and booklet groups did.

Figure 6.4: Parts of the information found most interesting for the different formats

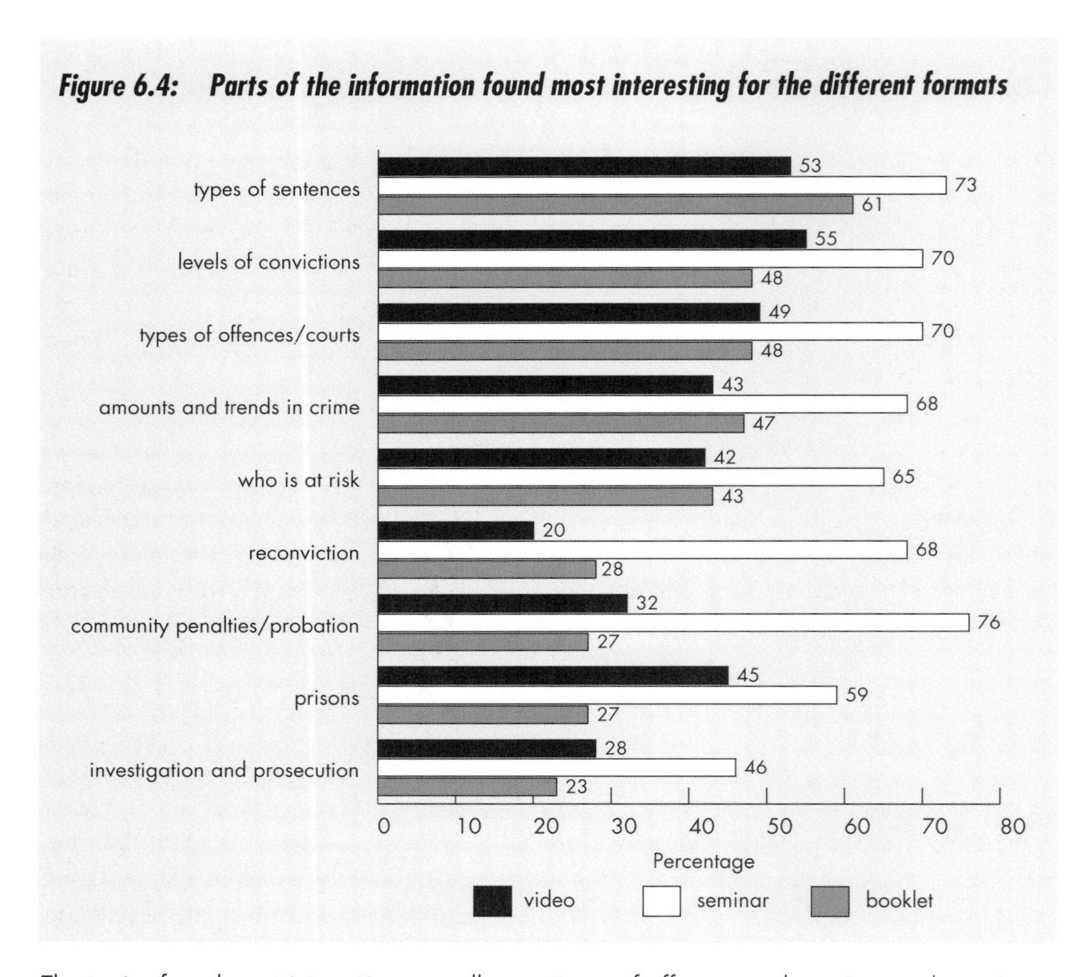

The topics found most interesting overall were types of offences and court procedures, types of sentences, levels of convictions, and amounts and trends in crime. Of least interest was the information given about investigation and prosecution.

The prison part of the booklet was rated as much less interesting than the corresponding parts of the video or seminar. It is likely this was at least partly due to the video including footage of a prison and some interviews with prisoners, and the seminar including a presentation from a prison governor. Those attending the seminars were much more likely to have found the information about community penalties and probation interesting than those reading the booklet or watching the video, perhaps due to the presence of a probation officer at the seminars. The seminar group was also much more likely to have found the information about rates of reconviction interesting, perhaps because the presence of probation officers tended to prompt discussion of this topic.

Accuracy of the information

When rating the information sources on the biased/unbiased scale, the average rating for the booklet and seminars was about 4 (ratings were between 1 and 5, with 5 being 'unbiased'). The video was rated as being a little more biased at 3.5. Similarly, for ratings on whether the formats were thought to be propaganda or factual, all three sources were rated on average about 4 out of 5, where 5 was 'factual' and 1 'propaganda'. There was some mention of bias in response to open questions, particularly from the seminar and video groups, but not many people felt this.

Around a third of those in the seminar and video groups said there were things they did not believe, or disagreed with in the information presented to them. This figure was lower for the booklet at only 15 per cent. The most commonly mentioned things that participants said they did not believe or disagreed with were firstly that the crime rate is falling, and secondly the number of 40-year-old men with criminal convictions. All the speakers at the seminars were thought to be highly accurate and convincing.

Learning and impact

Self-reported learning and information that was surprising

A majority of participants (75%) reported being surprised by what they learnt from the information sources. People were consistently surprised across most socio-demographic groups. Fewer of the booklet group reported being surprised by anything they learnt than the other groups.

The information that participants in the booklet group said they were most surprised by included the low rates of victimisation of older age groups, the fact crime is falling, the cost of a prison place, and that a third of men have a conviction by the age of 40. Reactions to these facts were mixed. Some respondents said they were surprised that some of the sentences did not seem long enough, and that community sentences were lenient. However, others were surprised that offenders were supervised so much by the probation service, and that sentences were longer than they thought. One respondent made the link in their response between the cost and effectiveness of sentences:

'...that prison cost more than a community penalty – a lot more, but made no difference in the re-offending rate.'

Similar comments were made by the seminar and video groups. The seminar group also mentioned the effort put into reducing re-offending by the probation service. The comments from the video group included some on the footage of prisoners. Most of these were either expressing surprise that the prisoners seemed ordinary and articulate, or that the prisoners were criticising the prison regime.

All but two of the participants reported learning at least something from the information they had received and 55 per cent said they learnt a lot. Those from social classes A and B were more likely to say they had learnt a lot and those who had read a tabloid newspaper in the last week were less likely to say so. The percentage saying they had learnt a lot was highest for the seminar (73%) and lowest for the booklet (46%).

The booklet presented the information in a more concise way, and contained less information overall (concentrating primarily on that required to answer the 'quiz' questions), so it is unsurprising that the participants were not so surprised and felt they learnt less.

There appears to be a relationship between being surprised and the perceived amount learnt. This is consistent with the theory of Parrott (1995) discussed in chapter 1 who suggests that a discrepancy between expectations and reality is one way active processing can be promoted. People who reported being surprised by what they learnt were significantly more likely to say they learnt a lot than those who said they were not surprised. Breaking down by information type, this difference is significant for the booklet and video groups. The seminar group were all likely to say they had learnt a lot (Figure 6.5).

Figure 6.5: Percentage who were or were not surprised by what they learnt who said they learnt a lot, by information type.

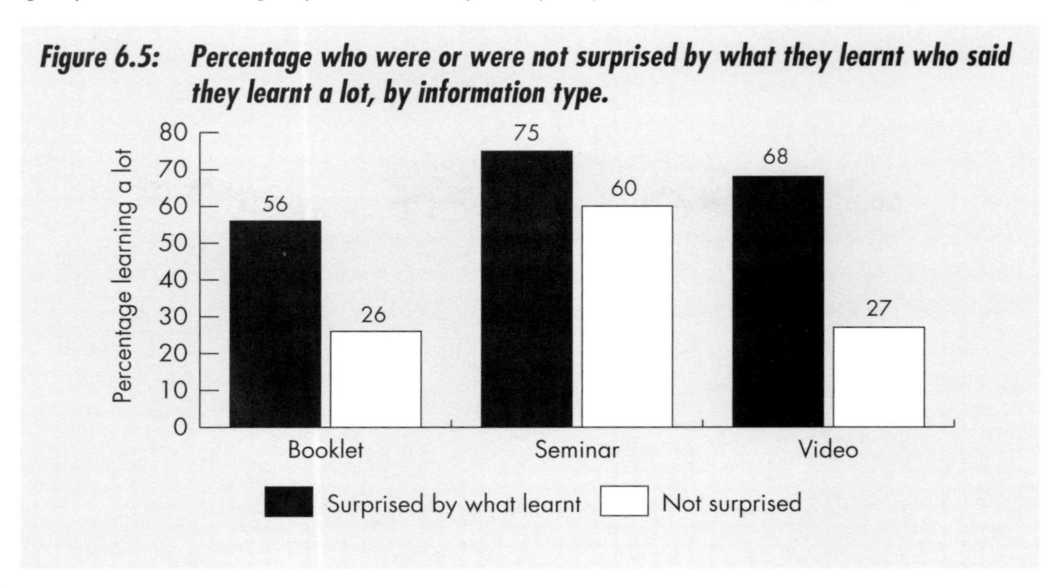

This relationship seems to apply to individual types of information. Many of the items of information which were said to be most surprising were also those where most improvement in knowledge is seen (chapter 4), particularly crime trends and the cost of prison.

Changing views

44 per cent of respondents said they had changed their views as a result of the information they had been given, with those with qualifications and those aged under 45 more likely to say this. Participants who thought they had learnt a lot were also significantly more likely to report having changed their opinions. Almost three-quarters of the seminar group said they had changed their views, compared with 41 per cent of the booklet group and 32 per cent of the video group (Figure 6.6).

On average participants in all groups reported that they were somewhat more confident in the CJS as a result of the information they had received. This is one of the only questions where the seminar was not rated the most highly. This is consistent with the findings reported in chapter 5 for the confidence measures as the seminar had less of an impact on confidence than the other information types.[33]

Figure 6.6: Percentage of participants who said they changed their views as a result of what they learnt.

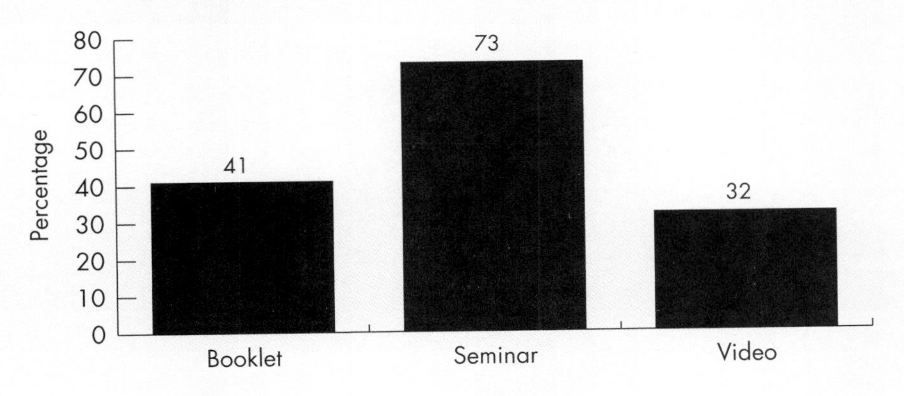

33. There were no significant changes in confidence on any of the measures for the seminar group.

How could the information formats be improved?

Although all the information sources were rated highly by participants, there were a number of areas identified for improvement.

Some participants in the booklet group thought that some of the colours were difficult to read, and that sometimes the statistics were hard to understand. However, others thought that it should go into more detail in a few of the topic areas. Those who saw the video thought that it could be improved by breaking up some of the long segments of film of the seminar and including more footage of prison and prisoners, as well as interviews with victims. The main suggestion given for the seminar was that it should be made longer to allow fuller discussion. Some of those who attended the seminar said they would have liked a written summary.[34]

Conclusion

Generally, ratings of all the information sources were positive. All of the information formats were thought to be informative, interesting, enjoyable and helpful, with the seminar the most positively rated on nearly all of the evaluation questions. The booklet and video were both judged to be 'modern', and 'different' from other government publications. All the formats were generally thought to be credible and accurate, although this was less so for the video. Participants expressed surprise at many of the facts presented, and this was associated with greater self-reported learning. Respondents from all the groups said that they had changed their views and many thought they were now more confident about the system.

34. This was not provided at the time as it would have confused the impact of the seminar with that of the written material. However, participants in both the seminar and video groups were provided with a copy of the booklet after their follow-up interview.

7 Discussion and conclusions

Providing simple factual information can improve public knowledge about crime and sentencing in the short term at least. Participating in the project also had an impact on attitudes to and confidence in the CJS. After being given information about crime and criminal justice system procedures and practices, participants were (on average): less worried about being the victim of crime; less likely to say sentencing is currently too lenient; and, had more confidence that it is effective in bringing people who commit crimes to justice, and respects the rights of the accused. Each of the three information formats tested (the booklet, seminar and video) improved knowledge and had some influence on attitudes.

Using information to improve knowledge

National Statistics, which has a code of practice that many Home Office Research Development and Statistics Directorate publications are subject to, has a stated aim of providing a window on the work and performance of government. Most National Statistics publications are not, however, aimed at the general public. Even the more 'user friendly' formats that have been developed, such as the *Digest of Information on the criminal justice system in England and Wales* (Barclay & Tavares (eds) 1999) and the *Guide to the criminal justice system in England and Wales* still require quite a high level of literacy and/or numeracy.

Previous research had shown that levels of knowledge about crime and the CJS in the general population are very poor and that those with the poorest level of knowledge are also likely to be those with the lowest levels of literacy and understanding.[35] For this reason, the information participants were provided with was deliberately kept to a minimum. The complexities of the criminal justice and legal system were necessarily simplified to convey general principles. There is of course no 'right' answer as to the level of detail to include. Finding a reasonable compromise between keeping the message simple and not misrepresenting the facts is itself a challenge. But, as even at this relatively simple level no one who took part could correctly answer all the knowledge questions, we were reassured that there was still further material that could have been absorbed.

35. See Hough and Roberts (1998) and Mattinson and Mirrlees-Black (2000).

Despite the simple style of the messages presented, and the range of methods (written, aural and visual) used to convey the material, it was the better educated who were best at absorbing and recalling the information in the survey context. However, even those with less demonstrated experience of learning whose initial level of knowledge was particularly poor did show a marked improvement. It is important to be aware, therefore, that some people are more responsive to improving knowledge than others, particularly those with educational qualifications. Alternative strategies may be necessary to improve the knowledge of those without these advantages.

Using information to change attitudes

Although there were marked improvements in attitudes to the CJS, there was little evidence that the shifts in attitudes found here could be attributed solely to improved knowledge about crime and criminal justice. The sheer act of engaging people in this type of exercise appears to be sufficient to bring about an improvement in attitudes. Despite our preconceived belief that those with extreme views were likely to be the most intransigent, for all three of these attitudes, this was the group who were the most likely to change their minds. It may be that those with the most extreme views are those in most need of reassurance that the state is acting in their best interests.

Participants' beliefs about the aims of sentencing did not change much after receiving information, but they were already focussed on crime reduction and arguably the way the material was presented – measuring effectiveness of disposals in terms of reduction in re-offending rates for instance – was unlikely to have influenced this view. Choice of sentences for offenders also did not change much, but again this is hardly surprising given the initial preference for non-custodial sentences.

The format of information

All three formats were well received by those taking part in the research. All three produced similar improvements in knowledge, and although there were different patterns on the attitudinal measures, all showed some improvements. The key distinction between them, though, was the extent to which they reached their potential audience.

Participation in the seminar was very low, despite the fact that participants were being paid to attend. Many of those who initially agreed to attend did not turn up at the venues, and those that did were not at all representative of the general population. They were more likely to have a prior interest in the subject matter, to have educational qualifications and to read broadsheet newspapers. Although the seminar received particularly positive ratings – perhaps reflecting participants' greater involvement – it may be that this group would have been equally as enthusiastic about the other formats. We have to conclude that seminars are unlikely to be an effective way of conveying this type of information to a wide cross-section of the general public.

The effectiveness of the video in this respect is more difficult to judge, because there was a particularly poor response rate to the follow-up survey for the video group. We cannot rule out the possibility that this was because respondents had not got around to watching it by the time the interviewer called.

The booklet was read by the greatest proportion of those it was offered to. Reflecting this, those who read it were fairly representative of the general public in composition.

The booklet also scores highly on cost-effectiveness. The seminars were the most expensive because they incurred venue and travel costs. They also required a significant time input on behalf of presenters. The booklet and video on the other hand initially incurred design costs, and then production and distribution costs. But the per participant cost would decrease significantly over time with the booklet becoming cheaper on a copy by copy basis than the video format. However, technological advances may make the delivery of audio-visual material, to personal computers for instance, a viable method in the future.

Next steps

Improving public confidence in the criminal justice system is one of the key aims of the three government departments involved in criminal justice. Given the improvements in confidence demonstrated here, providing information to the public might prove an important element of this work alongside initiatives to improve the system itself. Initiatives have tended to concentrate on improving satisfaction and confidence in the criminal justice system amongst victims, witnesses and those in contact with the system. However, clearly there is widespread dissatisfaction and misunderstanding of the system amongst the general public that also needs to be addressed.

One of the conclusions reached by the review of the sentencing framework in the *Making Punishments Work* report, using evidence from this research, was that there was no need to change the levels of punishment purely to increase public confidence. Instead it suggested that better and more accessible information for the public was needed, and it recommended that the Home Office should consider ways of increasing public knowledge about how sentencing is intended to work and how it is working in practice.

For those groups in contact with the CJS, dissemination is fairly straightforward. For instance, material can be left with courts and victim support organisations. The contact itself is likely to be sufficient to prompt interest in and engagement with the information.

It is more difficult to identify methods for disseminating material to those with no contact, or indeed, no particular interest in the CJS. To absorb this sort of information, interest in the subject matter needs to be raised. Law and order issues seem to be a subject where a relatively high level of interest already exists, so all that might be required is a way of tapping into this existing interest. Social surveys, news articles, and prize quizzes are the kinds of methods that are likely to be successful.

An information marketing campaign would therefore have a number of different strands – targeting groups of witnesses, victims and jurors through existing contacts with the CJS, alongside a proactive information campaign targeted at the general public.

The booklet is currently the most cost-effective of the formats tested and it also reached the widest cross-section of people. For this reason the booklet has been updated and redesigned, taking into account the comments from the participants in the research. If it is well received it will be revised periodically and will form part of the strategy to improve confidence in the criminal justice system in England and Wales.

Appendix A Methodology and statistical significance

Sampling error and statistical significance

In any sample survey or research, the sample may produce results that differ from the figures that would have been obtained if the whole population had taken part in the research. This is called *sampling error*. Sampling error means that changes or differences found may have occurred by chance. Tests of *statistical significance* are used to identify which changes are unlikely to have occurred by chance. Where a test has found a result to be significant at the 5% level ($p<0.05$) there is only a one in 20 chance that this result is due to chance variation.

Weighted data

In this research, the raw data from the general public survey (GPS) have been adjusted to correct for imbalances in sampling which affect the representativeness of the sample. The participant data have not been weighted.

Interviewing method

The interviews were conducted using Computer Assisted Personal Interviewing (CAPI) where the questionnaire responses are entered directly on to a portable computer by the interviewer and took an average of 31 minutes in the first stage, and 44 minutes in the second stage. The questionnaire was piloted before the first stage, with ten respondents in two towns. This led to some minor revisions. Interviewers were provided with instructions for the interview and the recruitment to the second stage. The interviews were carried out in the afternoon and evening, and at weekends to help make sure the sample included people who worked.

Sample design

The aim in the first stage was to obtain a representative sample of the general public aged 16 or over. The sample was clustered because of the need for seminar participants to be within a reasonable distance of the venue. Sampling points were selected systematically, stratified by region and social class. Respondents were selected randomly, using systematic selection of sampling points stratified by region and social class. Postcode sectors were then selected within the sampling points. The data were weighted to the population by region for analysis.

Quotas were used to ensure that the groups receiving the different information sources were well balanced. The participants received financial incentives to take part. Those in the seminar groups received £40, plus travelling expenses. Those who read the booklet or watched the video received £20 each.

Design of the questionnaire

Two versions of the questionnaire were used – one for the before stage and general public survey, and the second for after participants had received information in one of the three formats. Much of the content of the two versions was the same and included open-ended as well as closed questions and covered confidence in the criminal justice system, awareness of sentences, sentencing scenarios, aims of sentencing, aggravating and mitigating factors in sentencing, knowledge questions about the CJS and demographic questions. The questionnaire found at http://www.homeoffice.gov.uk/rds/horspubs1.html combines both versions to include all the questions asked. Most of the items were closed questions, but there were a number of open-ended questions for which the interviewers used Pen CAPI to note the responses.

Appendix B

Booklet

Catching up
with crime and
sentencing

The full version of this booklet can be found at http://www.homeoffice.gov.uk/rds/horspubs1.html

Appendix C
Additional tables

Table C4.1: Take up rates for the three information formats

		Number	% agreeing to participate	% recontacted	% who had read/ watched/ attended
Booklet	Those asked to take part	195	72	58	56
	Those who agreed to participate	141	100	80	77
	Those recontacted	113	-	100	96
	Those who had read/watched/attended	109	-	-	100
Seminar	Those asked to take part	319	36	12	12
	Those who agreed to participate	116	100	32	32
	Those recontacted	37	-	100	100
	Those who had read/watched/attended	37	-	-	100
Video	Those asked to take part	188	74	41	39
	Those who agreed to participate	139	100	55	53
	Those recontacted	77	-	100	96
	Those who had read/watched/attended	74	-	-	100

Table C5.1: Percentage of respondents reporting reduced worry after receiving information (not including those originally 'not at all worried')

	N Total = 213	% reduced worry	Sig at p<0.05 level
Sex			
male	103	28	
female	110	21	
Age			
16-34	60	23	
35-64	125	24	
65+	28	29	
Class			
AB	60	22	
C1	57	28	
C2	42	33	
DE	54	17	
Ethnicity			
White	208	25	
Not white	5	20	
Qualifications			
Some	176	27	
None	37	11	*
Victim of crime			
Has been a victim	141	25	
Hasn't been a victim	72	24	
Original level of fear			
Very worried	37	54	
Fairly worried	87	28	*
Not very worried	89	9	*
Interest in law and order issues			
Very interested in law and order	79	33	*
Fairly or less interested in law and order	134	19	
Original level of knowledge			
Less than 6 correct	189	25	
6 or more correct	24	17	
Information source			
Booklet	108	19	
Seminar	35	40	*
Video	70	17	
Change in knowledge			
Not increased knowledge	60	22	
Increased knowledge	153	26	

Table C5.2: Percentage becoming less punitive after receiving information (only those thinking sentencing a little or much too lenient in first survey)

	N Total = 159	% more satisfied	Sig at p<0.05 level
Sex			
male	75	31	
female	80	40	
Age			
16-34	35	37	
35-64	96	32	
65+	24	46	
Class			
AB	40	38	
C1	39	31	
C2	36	36	
DE	40	38	
Ethnicity			
White	152	36	
Not white	3	33	
Qualifications			
Some	124	39	
None	31	23	
Victim of crime			
Has been a victim	55	36	
Hasn't been a victim	100	35	
Original beliefs about sentencing			
Much too lenient	98	29	
A little too lenient	57	47	*
Interest in law and order issues			
Very interested in law and order	60	37	
Fairly or less interested in law and order	95	35	
Original level of knowledge			
Less than 6 correct	134	36	
6 or more correct	21	33	
Information source			
Booklet	79	38	
Seminar	24	38	
Video	52	31	
Change in knowledge			
Not increased knowledge	48	25	
Increased knowledge	107	40	

Table C5.3: Percentage becoming more confident that the CJS brings people who commit crimes to justice (not including those very confident in first survey)

	N Total = 216	% more confident	Sig at p<0.05 level
Sex			
male	105	34	
female	110	36	
Age			
16-34	59	37	
35-64	127	33	
65+	29	38	
Class			
AB	61	38	
C1	57	32	
C2	41	34	
DE	56	36	
Ethnicity			
White	210	35	
Not white	5	40	
Qualifications			
Some	177	33	
None	38	42	
Victim of crime			
Has been a victim	141	34	
Hasn't been a victim	74	37	
Original level of confidence			
Fairly confident	80	6	
Not very confident	108	44	*
Not at all confident	27	85	*
Interest in law and order issues			
Very interested in law and order	78	33	
Fairly or less interested in law and order	137	36	
Original level of knowledge			
Less than 6 correct	190	37	
6 or more correct	25	20	
Information source			
Booklet	106	33	
Seminar	37	30	
Video	72	40	
Change in knowledge			
Not increased knowledge	57	32	
Increased knowledge	158	36	

References

Anderson, S., Ingram, D. and Hutton, N. (2002). *Public attitudes towards sentencing and alternatives to imprisonment.* SP Paper 537. London: HMSO.

Barclay, G. and Tavares, C. (eds) (1999). *Digest 4: Information on the criminal justice system in England and Wales.* London: Home Office.

Doble, J. (1997). Survey shows Alabamians Support Alternatives. In M. Tonry and K. Hatlestad (eds) *Sentencing Reform in Overcrowded Times: A comparative perspective.* Oxford: Oxford University Press.

Doble & Immerwahr (1997). Delawareans Favor Prison Alternatives. In M. Tonry & K. Hatlestad (eds) *Sentencing Reform in Overcrowded Times: A comparative perspective.* Oxford: Oxford University Press.

Fishkin, J.S. (1996). Bringing Deliberation to Democracy. *The Public Perspective* Vol. 7. No.1. pp. 1-4.

Furnham, A. Gunter, B. and Green, A. (1990). Remembering Science: the Recall of Factual Information as a Function of the Presentation Mode. *Applied Cognitive Psychology,* 4, pp. 203-212.

Halliday, J. (2001). *Making Punishments Work: Report of a review of the Sentencing Framework for England and Wales.* London: Home Office.

Home Office (2000). *A guide to the criminal justice system in England and Wales.* London: Home Office.

Hough, M. (1996). *People talking about punishment.* The Howard Journal Vol. 35 No.3. pp. 191-214.

Hough, M. and Moxon, D. (1985). Dealing with offenders: Popular opinion and the views of victims, findings from the British Crime Survey. *The Howard Journal* Vol. 24. No.3. pp. 160-175.

Hough, M. and Roberts, J. (1998). *Attitudes to punishment: findings from the British Crime Survey.* Home Office Research Study No.179. London: Home Office.

Hough, M. and Roberts, J. (1999). Sentencing trends in Britain: Public knowledge and public opinion. *Punishment and Society: The International Journal of Penology* Vol. 1. No.1. pp. 11-26.

Kay, A. F. (1996). How the questionnaire could have been improved. *The Public Perspective* Vol. 7. No.3. pp. 20-22.

Ladd, E.V. (1996). Magic Town: Jimmy Stewart demonstrates the "Hawthorne Effect". The *Public Perspective* Vol. 7. No.3. pp. 16-17.

Mattinson, J. and Mirrlees-Black, C. (2000). *Attitudes to Crime and Criminal Justice: Findings from the 1998 British Crime Survey.* Home Office Research Study No. 200. London: Home Office.

Mirrlees-Black, C. (2001). *Confidence in the Criminal Justice System: Findings from the 2000 British Crime Survey.* Home Office Research Findings No.137. London: Home Office.

O'Keefe, G.J., Rosenbaum, D.P., Lavrakas, P.J., Reid, K. and Botta, R.A. (1996). *Taking a bite out of crime: The impact of the National Citizens' Crime Prevention Media Campaign.* Thousand Oaks, CA: Sage.

Parrott, R.L. (1995). Motivation to attend to Health Messages. In Maibach, E. and Parrot, R.L. *Designing Health Messages.* London: Sage.

Riley, D. and Mayhew, P. (1980). *Crime Prevention Publicity: an assessment.* Home Office Research Study No. 63. London: HMSO.

Russell, N and Morgan, R. (2000). *Sentencing Domestic Burglary.* Sentencing Advisory Panel Research Report 1.

Tarling, R. and Dowds, L. (1997). 'Crime and Punishment'. In Jowell *et al* (eds) *British Social Attitudes, the 14th Report.* Aldershot: Ashgate.

RDS Publications

Requests for Publications

Copies of our publications and a list of those currently available may be obtained from:

Home Office
Research, Development and Statistics Directorate
Communication Development Unit
Room 275, Home Office
50 Queen Anne's Gate
London SW1H 9AT
Telephone: 020 7273 2084 (answerphone outside of office hours)
Facsimile: 020 7222 0211
E-mail: publications.rds@homeoffice.gsi.gov.uk

alternatively

why not visit the RDS website at
Internet: http://www.homeoffice.gov.uk/rds/index.html

where many of our publications are available to be read on screen or downloaded for printing.